Hg2 New York

A Hedonist's guide to
New York

Written by Andrew Stone
Photographed by Pascal Perich

A Hedonist's guide to New York

Managing director — Tremayne Carew Pole
Marketing director — Sara Townsend
Series editor — Catherine Blake
Design — Katy Platt
Maps — Amber Sheers
Repro — Dorchester Typesetting
Printers — Printed in China by Leo
Publisher — Filmer Ltd

Additional photographs by Andrew Stone; Noah Kalina (Momofoku Ssam); Robert Polidori (WD-50); Jason Howard (Pacha NYC); Spencer Tucker (Central Park in Fall); Alan Batt (Telepan); Bill Bettencourt (Gramercy Tavern) and Gregory Goode (The Bowery Hotel).

Email — info@hg2.com
Website — www.hg2.com

First published in the United Kingdom in October 2007 by
Filmer Ltd
47 Filmer Road,
London SW6 7JJ

ISBN — 1-905428-07-3 / 978-1-905428-07-6

Hg2 New York

CONTENTS

How to…

A Hedonist's guide to New York is broken down into easy to use sections: Sleep, Eat, Drink, Snack, Party, Culture, Shop, Play, and Info. In each of these sections you will find detailed reviews and photographs. At the front of the book you will find an introduction to the city and an overview map, followed by introductions to the five main areas and more detailed maps. On each of these maps you will see the places that we have reviewed, laid out by section, highlighted on the map with a symbol and a number. To find out about a particular place simply turn to the relevant section, where all entries are listed alphabetically. Alternatively, browse through a specific section (e.g. Eat) until you find a restaurant that you like the look of. Next to your choice will be a coloured box – each colour refers to a particular area of the city. Simply turn to the relevant map to discover the location.

Updates

Hg2 have developed a network of journalists in each city to review the best hotels, restaurants, bars, clubs, etc., and to keep track of the latest developments – new places open up all the time, while others simply fade away or just go out of style. To access our free updates as well as the content of each guide, simply log onto our website www.Hg2.com and register. We welcome your help. If you have any comments or recommendations, please feel free to email us at info@hg2.com.

Book your hotel on Hg2.com

We believe that the key to a great city break is choosing the right hotel. Our unique site now enables you to browse through our selection of hotels, using the interactive maps to give you a good feel for the area as well as the nearby restaurants, bars, sights, etc., before you book. Hg2 has formed partnerships with the hotels featured in our guide to bring them to readers at the lowest possible price. Our site now incorporates special offers from selected hotels, as well as a diary of interesting events taking place, "Inspire Me."

The concept

A Hedonist's guide to… is designed to appeal to a more urbane and stylish traveler. The kind of traveler who is interested in gourmet food, elegant hotels and seriously chic bars – the traveler who feels the need to explore, shop, and pamper themselves away from the crowds.

Our aim is to give you an insider's knowledge of a city, to make you feel like a well-heeled, sophisticated local, and to take you to the most fashionable places in town to rub shoulders with the local glitterati.

In today's world work rules our life, and weekends away are few and far between; when we do manage to get away we want to have as much fun and to relax as much as possible with the minimum amount of stress. This guide is all about maximizing time. There is a photograph of each place we feature, so before you go you know exactly what you are getting into; choose a restaurant or bar that suits you and your needs.

We pride ourselves on our independence and our integrity. We eat in all the restaurants, drink in all the bars, and go wild in the nightclubs – all totally incognito. We charge no one for the privilege for appearing in the guide, and every place is reviewed and included at our discretion.

We feel cities are best enjoyed by soaking up the atmosphere: wander the streets, indulge in some retail therapy, re-energize yourself with a massage and then get ready to eat like a king and party hard on the local scene.

New York

Welcome to New York City – the 'Big Apple', the 'Melting Pot', 'Gotham', 'Empire City', the 'City that Never Sleeps' and what we affectionately call the 'City That's Seen It All'. And we're not talking in a tired, old prostitute way. We're talking a true cradle of culture, the world's greatest walking city where citizens of every nation – speaking every tongue – come to find their place and prosper. It's a place where excellence – in terms of art, business, media, finance, fashion… everything – is not just a possibility, it's an expectation. If you touch down in this frenetic burg and give it a fair shot, it might just change your life. But if you come expecting a metallic version of your home-town, you're better off taking your hard-earned vacation dollars and hitting some lower impact city like Allentown, Pennsylvania, a.k.a. 'Cement City', or better yet a Club Med.

Comprised of five boroughs – the Bronx, Brooklyn (below), Manhattan, Queens, and Staten Island – New York City is the most densely popu-lated city in world, with over 8.1 million residents pounding its pave-ment, causing its neighborhoods to change like water over rock, and indulging in the purity of its seasons. (Winter here means heavy coats and slushy sidewalks; summer means breaking a sweat and taking

refuge in air conditioned cabs and boutiques. Spring is out of a story-book, and the autumn – with its fallen leaves on the parks and stoops and cool, mollifying breeze – offer its citizens a reminder every day how lucky they are to have landed here.) There are many different kinds of cities overlapping one another all the time… It's the New York of Woody Allen films as much as it is that of Edith Wharton novels. The traders on Wall Street, the vendors along Canal Street, the gallerists of Chelsea, the socialites of the Upper East Side, the restaurateurs, cab drivers, shop owners, Broadway performers, tycoons, artists,

authors… Each person has a distinct story to tell, one that could only have come to life here.

As far as the good life goes, there is no finer place to chase down your dreams or indulge your fantasies. Countless restaurants, *boites*, and shops are yours for the discovering… Neighborhoods boast their own distinctive charms, and the fact that everyone walks everywhere makes it the most interactive place you're likely to experience. Those who think it's only about Times Square and Midtown's skyscrapers need to cover some more territory – hit the cobblestone in the West Village, cozy up in a Nolita café, roll in Central Park's grass, or take in the sunset over the Hudson River at the 79th Street Boast Basin. It's a lot to take in – especially on your first visit – but you can handle it! Welcome to New York City, a place where you fit in, no matter who you are.

EAT

1. Applewood
2. Bouillabaisse
3. Frankie's 457
4. Sweetwater

 PARTY

6. Bembe
7. Black Betty
8. Riverside Church

0   500m   1km

MIDTOWN WEST

LINCOLN
CENTER

CLINTON

CHELSEA

TIMES
SQUARE

EAST VILLAGE
FASHION
DISTRICT

MIDTOWN
SOUTH

CHELSEA

FLATIRON

WEST
VILLAGE

GRAMERCY
PARK

UNION
SQUARE

GREENWICH
VILLAGE

HOUSTON STREET & BELOW
SOHO   NOHO

LITTLE
ITALY

TRIBECA

CHINATOWN

BATTERY
PARK
CITY

CIVIC
CENTER

LOWER
EAST SIDE

TWO
BRIDGES

FINANCIAL
DISTRICT

12

14

13

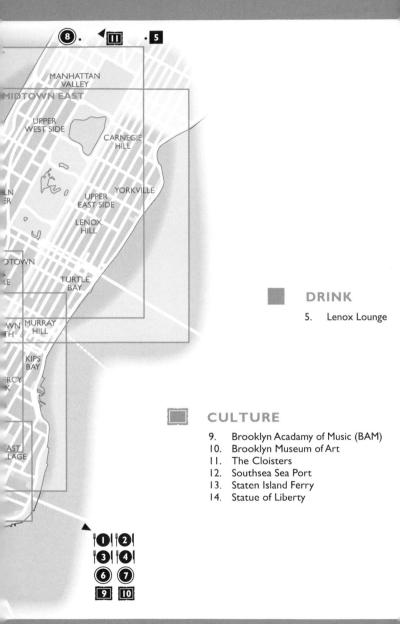

DRINK

5. Lenox Lounge

CULTURE

9. Brooklyn Acadamy of Music (BAM)
10. Brooklyn Museum of Art
11. The Cloisters
12. Southsea Sea Port
13. Staten Island Ferry
14. Statue of Liberty

Midtown West and the Upper West Side

There's a reason why, upon the mention of New York, most out-of-towners picture the following: Times Square's neon, the monolithic skyscrapers of Avenue of the Americas (also known as Sixth Avenue), Rockefeller Center's ice skaters, Carnegie Hall's majesty, the Rockettes' high kicks, Lincoln Center's fairytale fountain (thank you, Moonstruck), and the hyperactive applause at the conclusion of a Broadway show.

This area – the west side of the city, from 42nd Street up to Harlem – offers residents and visitors a million ways to experience New York at its most pure, in all of its hyper metropolitan grandeur. The Theater District – which includes a thoroughly scrubbed, tourist-friendly Times Square – is frenetic and inspiring, with its myriad theaters offering flashy stage plays and musicals. Although at times it feels like a raw nerve, Times Square possesses an awe-inspiring energy that has to be felt, at least once. Here, you will also find an ever-increasing number of reputable restaurants, particularly as you continue west. The gay com-

munity has settled into this area, known as Hell's Kitchen, and inspired many new establishments — bars, eateries, coffee shops, boutiques - to roll out their awnings.

At 59th Street, a couple of blocks up from Carnegie Hall, you'll come upon Columbus Circle – America's first traffic circle – and the most recent landmark to grace the Manhattan skyline, the Time Warner Center. This striking complex, with its luxury shops and world-class cuisine, is definitely worth a visit.

Further west, you'll find majestic entertainment at the Lincoln Center, while up the park sits the marvelous American Museum of Natural History – an absolute blast for folks of all ages. Not to ignore the obvious, Central Park is there at your disposal – and if you get peckish as you traverse this marvelous expanse of green, the Central Park Boathouse or legendary Tavern on the Green (reserve first) will fit the bill nicely. Further up and west, it's all about gorgeous side streets, happy urban families, wider avenues, and – as you reach Morningside Heights, just above 100th Street – the Ivy League influence of Columbia University. Spanning the area, along the river, are the Hudson River Park and Riverside Park – you'll be wise to spend a little time there.

So, take our advice… When you want to sink your teeth into the Big Apple, head northwest, young travelers.

DRINK

SNACK

EAT

SHOP

Highway

Dimaggio

Riverside West

West

Joe

West End Avenue

West 79th St

West

Amsterdam 76th

Riverside Drive

Broadway

West 72nd Street

Hudson River

West End Avenue

28

Columbus

14

LINCOLN CENTER

66th St

Central Park

7

27

4 **16**

Central Pk

12

18

21

West 55th St

57th St

25

West Ave

9

37

35

17

22

2

West 53rd

15

Avenue

6

23

CLINTON

10th West

11th Avenue

12th West 49th St

3

45th Avenue

9th Avenue

20

MIDTOWN

Broadway

7th

8th

East West

31

3

42nd Street

34

TIMES SQUARE

Ave of the Americas

11

5th Avenue

1 **8**

Midtown West and the Upper West Side
local map

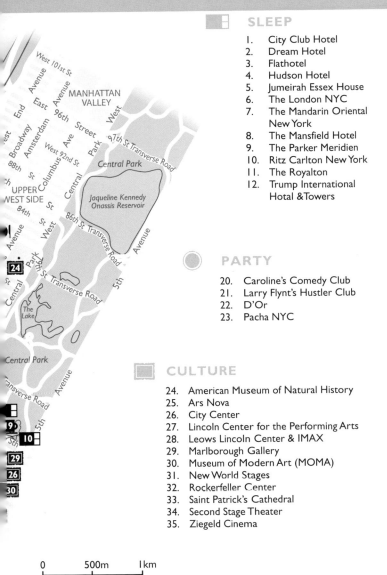

SLEEP

1. City Club Hotel
2. Dream Hotel
3. Flathotel
4. Hudson Hotel
5. Jumeirah Essex House
6. The London NYC
7. The Mandarin Oriental New York
8. The Mansfield Hotel
9. The Parker Meridien
10. Ritz Carlton New York
11. The Royalton
12. Trump International Hotal &Towers

PARTY

20. Caroline's Comedy Club
21. Larry Flynt's Hustler Club
22. D'Or
23. Pacha NYC

CULTURE

24. American Museum of Natural History
25. Ars Nova
26. City Center
27. Lincoln Center for the Performing Arts
28. Leows Lincoln Center & IMAX
29. Marlborough Gallery
30. Museum of Modern Art (MOMA)
31. New World Stages
32. Rockerfeller Center
33. Saint Patrick's Cathedral
34. Second Stage Theater
35. Ziegeld Cinema

Midtown East and the Upper East Side

Above 42nd Street on the east side of Fifth Avenue, the terrain begins to change... There's Grand Central Terminal and the confusing section of avenues that bend to accommodate it. Vanderbilt Avenue appears for a few blocks, Madison Avenue takes on a whole new feel, and Park Avenue becomes an extra wide thoroughfare with flower-rich medians separating the directions of traffic. Big business is everywhere – as is evidenced by the millions of suits that pound this pavement. The United Nations Headquarters is tucked off the east, right on the East River, as is the historic apartment complex Tudor City. As the 40s meet the 50s, Sutton Place appears along the river, as well – a swanky, exclusive stretch of park-flanked streets. Further up, where Midtown East becomes the Upper East Side, the Queensboro Bridge can be found as can the Roosevelt Island Tramway, which connects Manhattan to the two-mile long island community of Roosevelt Island.

Further to the center of the island, things get very hoity-toity. Ritzy doesn't begin to describe the Upper East Side – considered the most

concentrated pocket of wealth in the US, with the 10021 zip code being the most expensive real estate in the world – with its many museums, historic townhouses, prohibitively expensive restaurants, and dazzling shops within which you can blow lots and lots of money.

Featuring everything high-brow – restaurants like Daniel and Orsay; artistic institutions like the Whitney, the Met (right), and the Guggenheim; iconic private schools like Chapin and Dalton – the UES is seen as a bastion of gentility – particularly by its own well-funded residents. A rather beautiful neighborhood to stroll is Carnegie Hill, from the mid-80s through the 90s between Fifth and Third Avenues, with their gorgeous, single-family residences. Oh, and if you have an emergency in this hood, take comfort by the fact that half of the city's hospitals are close by.

Of course, a major element of the neighborhood's charms is Central Park. Upper East Siders love that they can call this sprawling, verdant expanse their "back yard." UES residents are constantly enjoying the park's bike trails, running paths, picturesque fountains, lakeside spots, concert series, playgrounds, and meadows. Particularly entertaining is the "meat market" scene in Sheep's Meadow that heats up as soon as summer temperatures arrive. A sea of sexy, single folk – or those who wish they were single – flock there to work on their tan lines, cavort, and flirt like mad people. If it's a hottie you're after, this is the place to scope out your options.

SLEEP

1. The Benjamin
2. The Carlyle
3. Dylan Hotel
4. The Library Hotel
5. Loews Regency Hotel
6. The Peninsula
7. The Pierre New York
8. Plaza Athenée
9. St. Regis
10. Waldorf Astoria

EAT

11. La Bilboquet
12. BLT Steak
13. Etats-Unis
14. Spigolo

SNACK

17. DU UT
18. Nespresso Boutique Bar

DRINK

15. Bemeimans Bar
16. Club Macanudo

Midtown East and the Upper East Side
local map

SHOP

29. Barney's New York
30. Bloomingdale's
    5th Avenue
    East 57th Street
    Madison Avenue

PARTY

19. Comic Strip Live
20. Scores

CULTURE

21. Cooper-Hewitt National Design Museum
22. The Frick Collection
23. Grand Central Terminal
24. Metropolitan Museum of Art
25. New York Public Library
26. Solomon R. Guggeheim Museum
27. United Nations
28. The Whitney Mueum of American Art

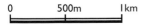

0   500m   1km

Chelsea, West Village, Meatpacking and Garment districts

One of the most beautiful sections of the city (save the Garment District, sorry to say), the western portion of Downtown above Houston Street and West of Fifth Avenue is known for its townhouses, art scene, campus life – as New York University does encircle historic Washington Square Park – and yuppie-acquired gay flourishes. (The gay community tends to doll up their 'hoods, thrive, then move on to the next spot when too many straight folks start horning in on their territory. These days, it's all about Hell's Kitchen.)

The West Village features a delightfully confusing maze of streets, some boasting cobblestone, and most offering incredible scenery – tree-lined, with brownstones and things like flags or window boxes (delightful!). These streets were paved in the early 1800s before the city's grid

plan was put into effect, and are an incredibly chic place to get lost. The neighborhood boasts the picturesque Abingdon Square and the High Line project (what will be an elevated green space on former elevated train tracks); and – at its westernmost point - the marvelous Christopher Street piers. The northern portion that bridges the West Village to Chelsea is the Meatpacking District – a formerly gritty section where animals died by day and trannies tricked

by night. But now, it houses pricey, trendy boutiques, hotels, and restaurants, and attracts tastemakers who love the irony of the locale.

Chelsea, meanwhile, is one of the most diverse charming areas in town, with its row houses, galleries, and fabled "Chelsea boys" (muscu-lar gay men who flock to Eighth Avenue and trade on the stereotypes of physical perfection, youthful attire, and house music). Chelsea Piers sits along the water, and numerous cafés and hotspots give the area a magnetic appeal.

To its north is the Garment District… the epicenter of the city's clothing industry and a very vital neighborhood that's coming a long way these days as Chelsea's influence expands north. Still, unless you're hitting Macy's, the Manhattan Mall, or Madison Square Garden, don't expect too much – although next year it could be a whole new story.

SLEEP

1. Bryant Park Hotel
2. Hotel Gansevoort
3. Maritime Hotel
4. Soho House New York

DRINK

14. Art Bar
15. Aspen
16. Barracuda
17. Black Door
18. Blind Tiger
19. Employees Only
20. Flatiron Lounge
21. Little Branch
22. The Otheroom
23. Temple Bar

SHOP

44. Macy's
- West 14th Street
- West 18th Street
- Bleecker Street
- Gansevoort Street
- Greenwich Avenue

SNACK

24. 202 Café
25. City Bakery
26. Florent
27. Joe
28. Rickshaw Dumpling Bar
29. Westville

EAT

5. 5 Ninth
6. Alta
7. Cookshop
8. Del Posto
9. Gin Lane
10. Mary's Fish Camp
11. Perry's Street
12. The Spotted Pig
13. Suenos

CULTURE

40. The Circle Line
41. The Joyce Theater
42. Lucille Lortel
43. Zach Feur Gallery

PARTY

30. APT
31. BB Kings Blues Club & Grill
32. Blue Note
33. Cielo
34. Comedy Cellar
35. Gotham Comedy Club
36. Hiro Ballroom
37. Marquee
38. Pink Elephant
39. The Plumm

0   500m   1km

Flatiron, Noho, and the East Village

Some say that you're either an "east side person" or a "west side person." While we love each half of the city equally, like the diplomatic parents of two very different children, the east side of Manhattan – particularly the East Village, Union Square, and the Flatiron District – possesses such unique, enlivening virtues that we can't help but beam with pride and pledge our allegiance.

As for the East Village – what is now an affluent expanse of personality-packed stores, eateries, and institutions used to be, well, dangerous, categorized by drug deals, seedy goings-on, and unbridled, raw artistic expression. A longtime haven for artists and musicians who moved east to "keep it real," this neighborhood housed some of the most legendary music clubs and bars – most of which have buckled under the pressure of skyrocketing rents. (R.I.P. CBGBs.) The scene along First and Second Avenues, not to mention around Alphabet City – Avenues A, B, C, and D, between 14th Street and Houston – is often electric, characterized by its alternative residents and boundary-pushing establishments. (Do note, however, that some of the city's very best cuisine can be found here, too.)

The East Village gives way to Union Square Park at 14th Street, bordered by Park Avenue South, Broadway, and 17th Street. Here, Manhattanites of every stripe check each other out, decompress, chow down, protest (many city protests and demonstrations start or end here), and – in sunnier months – chill out on the grass or the block-long stairs that face 14th Street. All the while, the city's hub of transportation exists underneath the park, connecting most of the city's subway lines. Then there is the famous greenmarket, a beloved outdoor emporium where we cityfolk get to sample and take home the finest produce, honey, breads, and flowers driven in from the rural areas. Do check out the famous George Washington statue, or chill out in Ghandi's Garden.

To its north, the Flatiron District – named for the historic triangular Flatiron Building at the intersection of 23rd Street, Fifth Avenue, and Broadway – is where many of the city's top furniture stores (such as ABC Carpet & Home) and printing houses reside, not to mention a host of chic businesses up and down Park Avenue South. To its east – at the northern point of beautiful Irving Place – the city's fabled, fenced-in private park, Gramercy Park, inspires envy in the passing masses without the privilege of a key. (Those are reserved for park-adjacent residents and guests of the Gramercy Park Hotel.) Further north is Murray Hill – running all the

way up to 42nd Street and Grand Central Station – with its many Indian establishments, the neighborhoods of Kips Bay and Tudor City, some noteworthy places to grab grub (Penelope on Lexington and 30th Street is adorable), and, of course, the Empire State Building.

SLEEP

1. The Bowery Hotel
2. Gramercy Park Hotel
3. Morgan's Hotel
4. The W Union Square

EAT

5. Degustation Wine & Tasting Bar
6. Gramercy Tavern
7. L'il Frankie's
8. Mercadito
9. Momofuku Ssam Bar

DRINK

10. Bar Veloce
11. Black & White
12. Bowlmor Lanes
13. d.b.a.
14. Heather's
15. Joe's Pub
16. Pegu Club
17. The Rose Bar
18. Zum Schneider

CULTURE

26. Empire State Building

Flatiron, Noho, and the East Village
local map

☕ SNACK

19. Caracas Arepa Bar
20. Casa Mono
21. Shake Shack

⊙ PARTY

22. China 1
23. Mr Black
24. Ten's World Class Cabaret
25. Webster Hall

🛍 SHOP

27. Bergdorf Goodman
28. Henri Bendel
29. Takashimaya
■   5th Avenue
■   Bond Street
■   Broadway
■   Union Square

0   500m   1km

Lower East Side, Nolita SoHo, Tribeca, Little Italy, and the Financial District

Welcome to Downtown Manhattan! There is so much to see, do, eat, smell, touch, and – yes – buy that we hardly know where to begin. Why not Houston Street, since that is the dividing line we've chosen. Houston (pronounced House-ton, not Hue-ston) Street is one of the city's busiest – and widest – thoroughfares in town, above which is NoHo (North of Houston) and below which is SoHo (South of Houston).

SoHo was the longtime artistic heart of the city, where the bohemian set seduced high society from their cheap, airy lofts. Nowadays, it's a prohibitively pricey nabe, off-limits to most everyone but the wealthiest or those lucky enough to find rent-stabilized apartments. Lined with designer shop after designer shop, it is one of the most attractive places to while away the hours in town, with plenty of expensive eateries to duck into with shopping bags in tow.

Nolita (North of Little Italy) borders SoHo to the east, starting at Lafayette Street, and essentially plays the role of SoHo's funkier younger sister. The boutiques and eateries here are artsier and more indie spirited, though don't be fooled into thinking that means less expensive. Little Italy used to be much larger, but now it's essentially a touristy strip of Mulberry Street. Sad. What was Little Italy is mostly now Chinatown, as that community has absolutely exploded – in fact it's the largest grouping of Chinese immigrants in the Western Hemisphere. Around Allen Street Chinatown gives way to what is known today as the Lower East Side, severely hip in its northern regions and slightly less gentrified to the south (though that changes by the second these days).

To SoHo's south and west is Tribeca (the Triangle Below Canal), a long-time industrial neighborhood that in recent years has become the go-to destination for monied hoity-toits who love the privacy and spa-cious real estate it provides. There are some great eateries and bars popping up all over the place, too. Then, at the southern tip of the island is the Financial District, Wall Street and such, home to Battery Park, South Street Seaport, the Stock Exchange, and some very cool architecture.

The street you live on – or even better, the street you shop and party on – really says a lot about you when you get down here. Mistakenly call a Nolita resident a SoHo resident and fire will flash in their eyes. God forbid you mistake Tribeca for the Financial District. And yes, there are edges on the Lower East Side that, without warning, will land you in the center of Chinatown. Do get a map, kids… but even then, be prepared to roll with the punches.

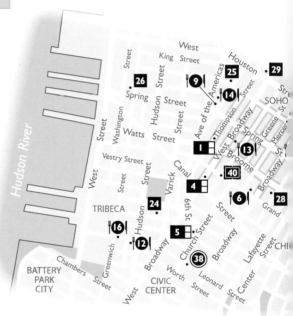

West Houston Street
King Street
West Street
Spring Street
Hudson River
Washington Street
Hudson Street
Watts Street
Vestry Street
West Street
Varick Street
Canal Street
6th St
Greenwich Street
Broadway
Worth Street
Leonard Street
Church Street
Broadway
Lafayette Street
Center Street
Grand Street
Spring Street
Broome Street
Greene St
Mercer St
Broadway
Ave of the Americas
West Broadway
Thompson Street
SOHO
St
Chambers Street

26 **9** **25** **29**
14
1 **13**
4 **40**
24 **6** **28**
16 **5**
12 **38**

TRIBECA
BATTERY PARK CITY
CIVIC CENTER
CHI

SHOP

- Elizabeth Street
- Broadway
- Broome Street
- Greene Street
- Lafayette Street
- Mercer Street
- Mott Street
- Mulberry Street
- Spring Street
- Thompson Street
- West Broadway

EAT

6. Antique Garage
7. Apizz
8. Balthazar
9. Blue Ribbon Sushi
10. Bread
11. Café Habana
12. Chanterelle
13. Cipriani Dowtown
14. Fiamma
15. Freemans
16. The Harrison
17. Little Giant
18. Prune
19. Public
20. Schiller's Liquor Bar
21. WD-50

SLEEP

1. 60 Thompson
2. Hotel on Rivington
3. The Mercer Hotel
4. Soho Grand
5. Tribeca Grand

PARTY

34. Bowery Ballroom
35. BLVD & Crash Mansion @ BLVD
36. The Box
37. Element
38. Knitting Factory

Hg2 New York

sleep...

No matter what kind of treatment you're used to at home, there's a fine-tuned, deluxe, delicious hotel experience tailor-made for you here in Manhattan. Having arrived at the nucleus of culture and commerce – harried and antsy – from wherever it is you hail, chances are you want nothing more than to nestle into a home base, drop your Louis Vuitton luggage, collapse across a sumptuous bed, splash a little water across your face, and plot your journey through New York from your spectacular view. Even if your luggage *doesn't* cost more than your college education, there's a place to tickle your fancy.

In this guide, we focused on many of the finer boutique properties plus some of the more legendary hotels like the St. Regis and the Waldorf Astoria, exploring their lobbies, guest rooms, and restaurants so you don't have to play the hit-or-miss game. While the task was difficult, we somehow managed to sleep our way through New York... and, whew, we are tuckered out! Here's a hint about them all, though – high thread count linens, fancy-pants toiletries, flat-screen TVs, and sexy staffs are pretty darn pervasive, so look at them for location, location, location and for an aesthetic style that suits you best. If you're here on business, the Bryant Park or the Morgans might the ticket for you. Feeling fashionable? Opt for the Mercer or Tribeca Grand. Need some pampering? Mandarin

Oriental at the Time Warner Center, all the way, baby. If you stay at the London NYC, maybe hothead chef-in-residence Gordon Ramsay will yell at you.

An exciting phenomenon of late is the presence of luxury hostelries in neigh-

borhoods best known for their grit. The Bowery Hotel, 3rd Street and the Bowery, is quite a departure from the vibe that long existed there… "Short stay" hotels were much more the norm on this block than celebrity-speckled hot spots. Then again, the chic, legendary Bowery Bar is just across the way, so it's not like you're in Siberia. Then there's the 21-floor, glass-encased Hotel on Rivington, on Rivington Street between Essex and Ludlow Streets, gleaming amidst the Lower East Side's tenement build-ings and hip eateries and bars. No one expected such a beacon to pop up there… or for it to become so popular!

Many of these hotels offer popular eateries and lounges; some have cabaret acts at venues such as Feinstein's and Café Carlyle. Others bring the glitzy local crowds straight to you, like the Soho Grand (above), the Gramercy Park Hotel (left), and the Dream. There's excitement if you want it; then again, there are delightful spots to rejuvenate and decompress from the hustle and bustle, like the Library (one of our absolute favorites) or Soho's secluded 60 Thompson. Kid's book heroine Eloise lives at the Plaza, while *Madeline* author and illustra-tor Ludwig Bemelmans provided the famous Central Park mural for the Carlyle Hotel's bar that bears his name. Some do Midtown, allowing for great access to the Great White Way (5th Ave) and all the business meetings that might bring you to town. Others serve as distinguishing beacons in trendy neighborhoods like the Lower East Side (the Hotel on Rivington) and the Meatpacking District (the Gansevoort or the Maritime). Where you stay will significantly impact the vibe of your trip, so do your research.

Do check the Hg2 website (www.hg2.com) for special packages and discount fares. It's not always the cheapest thing to stay here, but deals are there to be discovered all the time.

Our top 10 places to stay in New York are:
1. The Mandarin Oriental New York
2. Soho House New York
3. Gramercy Park Hotel
4. The Pierre New York
5. The Mercer Hotel
6. The Bowery Hotel
7. The Ritz Carlton New York
8. Plaza Athénée
9. St. Regis
10. City Club Hotel

Our top 5 for style are:
1. The Mandarin Oriental New York
2. The Bowery Hotel
3. The Gramercy Park Hotel
4. Hotel on Rivington
5. The Carlyle

Our top 5 for atmosphere are:
1. Soho House New York
2. The Mercer Hotel
3. The Bowery Hotel
4. The Gramercy Park Hotel
5. The Mandarin Oriental New York

Our top 5 for location are:
1. The Bryant Park Hotel
2. The Mandarin Oriental New York
3. Le Parker Meridien
4. Soho House New York
5. Hotel Gansevoort

60 Thompson, 60 Thompson Street (Broome), Soho
Tel: 877 431 0400   www.60thompson.com
Rates: $579–3,500

Owner Jason Pomeranc is cool, charming, and great to look at – and this relaxing hotel follows his example, with its 82 rooms and eight suites of slick, soothing luxury. Located mid-block on a sleepy stretch of West Soho – free from too many fawning passersby (a reason it's a favorite of many a

celebrity or fashion figure) – 60 Thompson features a top-notch Thai eatery, Kittichai, through the hotel's lobby, and a breathtaking roof lounge boasting an unobstructed 360-degree view of downtown called A60 (accessible only to hotel guests and VIPs with special gift memberships). Each room is decked with understated neutral tones, grand leather headboards, Sferra linens and towels, Fresh bath products, and minibar pantries stocked by haute grocery Dean & Deluca.

Style 8, Atmosphere 8, Location 8

The Benjamin, 125 East 50th Street (Lexington), Midtown
Tel: 212 715 2500   www.thebenjamin.com
Rates: $399–899

With over 100 guest rooms and 100 suites, this polished Eastside hostelry features a host of clever luxuries, including a sleep concierge (who walks you through 11 pillow choices), a "pampered pet" program for your four-legged travel companions, a spa featuring a host of relaxing therapies, and elegantly appointed living spaces. Originally the Hotel Beverly, constructed in 1927, the building itself is a throw-back to a gentler time, with its Gothic rose windows and dra-matic lobby. (Painter Georgia O'Keefe captured the Benjamin's beauty from her apartment across the way.) Staffers are exceedingly friend-ly, and the needs of both weary business travelers and romance-seeking couples are taken into serious considera-tion. The newly renovated Restaurant at the Benjamin is a notable, greenmarket-driven

new American spot; meanwhile the Emery Bar in the lobby draws a sophisti-cated crowd and serves up dolled-up comfort food such as rock shrimp spoonbread and lobster rolls. No one argues with the milk and cookies at turn-down.

Style 8, Atmosphere 8, Location 8

The Bowery Hotel, 335 Bowery (E 3rd St), Noho
Tel: 212 505 9100 www.theboweryhotel.com
Rates: $325–750

The most sought-after rooms of mid-2007 are located within this dramatic new hotel concept on the Bowery – a stretch historically known for its punk culture and flophouses. From the team behind the Meatpacking District's beloved Maritime hotel, the 17-story building brings a whole new clientele to the 'hood, who love its cool, bohemian atmosphere and very liv-able guest rooms (featuring hardwood floors, beamed ceilings, C.O. Bigelow bath products, oversized terrycloth robes, and plenty of up-to-the-minute gadgets such as iPod stereos and flat screens). Downstairs, the Lobby Bar packs in the sunglasses-at-night crowd who can't get enough of the expan-sive room done up in fancypants décor velvet antique couches, Persian rugs,

a classic marble fireplace, and unusual taxidermy. (Note the stuffed English bulldog… may he rest in peace.)

Style 9, Atmosphere 9, Location 7

The Bryant Park Hotel, 40 West 40th Street (6th), Midtown West
Tel: 212 869 0100   www.bryantparkhotel.com
Rates: $395–1000

For a truly chic stay, this handsome, modern boutique spot is located behind the New York Public Library, right on Bryant Park (as civilized a locale as you're likely to find along 42nd Street). Housed in the former American Radiator Building, it's a favorite of visiting fashion and media types, whose work has them bouncing in and out of this neighborhood at any moment.

The Bryant Park offers 107 guest rooms and 20 suites that overlook the park, all of which feature Egyptian cotton sheets, sound machines (for the insomniacs among us), high-definition flat-screen TVs, Tibetan rugs, and chic marble bathrooms. An on-site fitness center and the eponymous salon of celebrity hairstylist Ric Pepino keep you feeling fit and presentable among the oft-scantily clad crowd at its lobby restaurant, Koi, and the glitzy, pricey Cellar Bar.

Style 8, Atmosphere 8, Location 8

The Carlyle, 35 East 76th Street (Madison), Upper East Side
Tel: 212 744 1600 www.thecarlyle.com
Rates: $700–6,000

A city landmark that has been lovingly updated to appeal to today's finicky big-spending traveler, the 181-room Carlyle has catered to celebrities and giants of industry since its construction in 1930. It is recognized as a bastion of old-school style (its rooms were originally decorated by Dorothy Draper), though a modernizing touch-up by Mark Hampton and luxury suites from star designers Thierry Despont and Alexandra Champlimaud suggests that this grande dame doesn't shrink at the suggestion of change. (Despont is responsible for the chic, sleek feel of the lobby.) Rooms feature Yves Delorme comforters, 100% combed Egyptian Mako cotton linens,

 whirlpool tubs, marvelous antiques, Kiehls's toiletries, slipper and mono-grammed terry robes, iPod gear, and dreamy mini-bars stocked with Taittinger

Champagne, Dean & Deluca chocolates, and candy from Dylan's Candy Bar. (Many of the suites feature baby grand pianos.) Of course, its Café Carlyle is a cabaret mainstay, and Bemelmans Bar (see Drink) provides a cool, clubby retreat.

Style 9, Atmosphere 8, Location 9

City Club Hotel, 55 West 44th Street (6th), Midtown West
Tel: 212 921 5500 www.cityclubhotel.com
Rates: $225–795

Owned by obsessively private hotelier Jeff Klein, this pint-sized retreat – 65 rooms in all – is a dream for the incognito traveler, with its small lobby space free from excessive loiterers and plenty of high-end amenities that make guests feel right at home. Rooms were decorated by fashionable interior star Jeffrey Bilhuber, and master chef Daniel Boulud has kept crowds creatively fed at his acclaimed DB Bistro Moderne in the lobby. An exclusive

yet accessible vibe runs through the quiet property – a reflection of its regular monied clientele, of which hard-partying celebrities are intentionally absent. Frette linens, mahogany wood, chrome fixtures, and brown marble baths stocked with C.O. Bigelow products give each room a well-planned feeling of decadence, while a TV obscured by mirrors, carefully selected art collection, and original furniture give guests a true aesthetic treat.

Style 9, Atmosphere 9, Location 7

Dream Hotel, 210 West 55th Street (7th), Midtown West
Tel: 866-IDREAMNY; 212 247 2000 www.dreamny.com
Rates: $219–919

Hotelier Vikram Chatwal certainly must have been dreaming when he signed this quirky luxury boutique hotel into existence, and for that adventurous travelers can be grateful. His trippy lobby – outrageous with its two-story circular aquarium, avant-garde photography, Buddha statuary, and adjoined slender-but-sexy striped lounge – is reason enough to consider it for a night. But add in the crisp modernity of the 208 guestrooms and 20 suites – complete with futuristic workstations, large black leather headboards, chic white leather seating, and effervescent lighting – and the argument has been

made. As fantastical as the entrance is, the rooms are genuinely relaxing, and feature large plasma TVs, pre-loaded iPod audio players, 300-count Egyptian sheets, allergen-free feather beds, and super-soft bathrobes. The hotel's decadent restaurants Amalia and Serafina are perennially popular, and the bar D'Or in the basement is a hip downtown-style *boîte*. The Ava Lounge on the roof offers a comely waitstaff and panoramic views of Times Square and the Hudson. Meanwhile, the on-site Chopra Center and Spa from ohm master Deepak Chopra allows for a sybaritic break from the jet-set scene.

Style 8, Atmosphere 7, Location 8

Dylan Hotel, 52 East 41st Street (Madison), Midtown East
Tel: 212 338 0500 www.dylanhotel.com
Rates: $259–609

With its grand old marble staircase, soaring wood ceilings, transporting gothic feel, and cool, modern interior courtesy of designer Jeffrey Beers, this exceptional boutique hotel – steps from Grand Central – is housed within

the landmark Chemists Club of New York building, built in 1903 as a residence for a collective of noteworthy scientists. With its 107 rooms of Beaux Arts luxury, simplicity reigns supreme, with its muted tones, spacious work desks, luxurious Egyptian linens, Carrara marble bathrooms with basin sinks and walnut fixtures, and Gilchrist & Soames bath products. The Dylan's gorgeous Alchemy Suite was originally designed as a replication of a medieval laboratory (how cool is that?). Meanwhile, the cozy, cosseting Benjamin Steakhouse draws carnivorous crowds downstairs, with its roaring fireplace, vaulted ceilings, and decadent steaks for two, three, or four. (Yes, it's in the space that formerly housed Nyla, an eatery effort from Britney Spears. Ignore that.)

Style 9, Atmosphere 8, Location 7

Flatotel, 135 West 52nd Street (6th), Midtown West
Tel: 212 887 9400 www.flatotel.com
Rates: $409–850

For the sophisticated traveler who believes true comfort means feeling right at home, this 210-room, 70-suite tower is a breath of fresh air, complete with all the subdued, swank charms of flat-style living. (The building was originally built to introduce New Yorkers to the concept of British "flat" life, before morphing into its present hotel incarnation.) Contemporarily cool in its décor, with nary an expense spared, guests unwind from the moment

they drop their bags and curl up on its custom-made beds (decked, of course with high thread-count linens) or slump into Aeron desk chairs and gaze out at the striking views. Bathrooms features marble jacuzzi tubs and Gilchrist & Soames bath products, while kitchenettes, Sony Wega flat screen with Direct TV, and fresh flowers make each sizable unit extra livable. All the while, the chic, masculine lobby lounge boasts leather couches, a slate floor, and a splashy, cool scene. Guests receive complimentary access to the Athletic & Swim Club across the street (Olympic-size pool and all) and the resident restaurant, Moda – with its glass-top al fresco bar – serves up fashion-forward Italian fare.

Style 8, Atmosphere 8, Location 8

Gramercy Park Hotel, 2 Lexington Avenue (E 21st St), Gramercy Park
Tel: 212 920 3300   www.gramercyparkhotel.com
Rates: $595–5,000

Following an extensive overhaul, hotelier Ian Schrager unveiled his chic bohemian recasting of this landmark hotel in early 2007 to much acclaim – lauded as much for its bold, unlikely combination of stylistic elements as it has been for its relentlessly chic nightlife scene. Rich in artsy history – it sits in the space that was formerly architect Stanford White's home, before which it was the birthplace of Edith Wharton – the new Gramercy Hotel presents a dreamlike mixture of antique and contemporary pieces; its tiled-floor lobby, red velvet curtains, impressive fireplaces, and precious art sets a Wonderland-ish stage beneath its custom-made Venetian glass chandelier.

Artist Julian Schnabel lent his brilliance to its design, as well as to the Rose Bar and Jade Bar, which lure luminaries from the city's intelligentsia and jet set. Meanwhile, the chic roof bar – tended by a gorgeous staff – is available exclusively to hotel guests and special members. The hotel's 185 guest rooms and suites feature contrasting elements of grandeur and art-driven décor – spacious, colorful, and deluxe. The hotel's restaurant serves haute Chinese, and a state-of-the-art gym called Aerospace offers cutting-edge equipment.

Style 9, Atmosphere 9, Location 9

Hotel Gansevoort, 18 Ninth Avenue (W 13th St), Meatpacking District
Tel: 212 206 6700   www.hotelgansevoort.com
Rates: $555–925

Cool and cosseting, this tower is a symbol of the Meatpacking District's trendy charms and empties out onto the area's plentiful chic bars, restaurants, boutiques, and clubs. Its 166 rooms and 21 corner suites are eclectic and stylish, featuring bay window seating or balconies, plasma TVs, deluxe showers that double as steam rooms, feather beds topped by 400-thread-count Egyptian linens, and custom furniture. Among its myriad other offerings are a scenic heated rooftop pool (lit with ever-changing colored light and boasting spectacular river views), the Hiro Haraguchi hair salon, and world-class pampering at the Gansevoort Spa (think: three infinity-edged hydro pools, expert treatments, and a superior steam room). Guests can

work out at either the on-site fitness space or Clay, a luxury gym in the vicinity. All the while, glitzy types crowd into popular, multi-level Japanese eatery Ono (featuring both sushi and robata-style cuisine), grab nightcaps at O Bar, and take in the breeze of temperate summer nights in their al fresco garden lounge.

Style 8, Atmosphere 8, Location 9

Hotel on Rivington, 107 Rivington Street (Ludlow), Lower East Side
Tel: 212 475 2600   www.hotelonrivington.com
Rates: $325–700

In a first for the rapidly gentrifying Lower East Side – long known for its

tenements, alternative culture, and dingy urban authenticity – a prominent, glass-encased tower, 21 stories high, lures high-design enthusiasts, artistically inclined big spenders, and lovers of all things new and notewor-

thy to this unlikely neighborhood for a super-luxurious stay, complete with many feasts for the eyes. The Hotel on Rivington offers dramatic cityscapes through floor-to-ceiling windows, spacious guest rooms (many of which have balconies), and gorgeous interiors courtesy of Parisian interior designer India Mahdavi, who went for a tranquil, timeless look. Black or beige velvet sofas and chairs, Frette linen-topped Swedish Tempur-pedic mattresses, futuristic chrome tables, flat-screen TVs, two-person Japanese soaking tubs, glass-walled shower walls, pet-friendly floors, just scratch the surface of futuristic offerings (and there's a nice selection of wines in the minibar). The Italian mosaic Bisazza tile bathrooms – stocked with Ren of London products – are sleek and breathtaking. Luxury boutique Annie O. resides downstairs, as does the boundary-defying bistro Thor.

Style 9, Atmosphere 8, Location 7

Hudson Hotel, 356 West 58th Street (9th), Midtown West
Tel: 212 554 6000 www.hudsonhotel.com
Rates: $329–720

A great hotel is like the perfect woman... comforting, sexy, impeccably maintained, and totally fine with your leaving for good the next morning. Just kidding... though it's these traits and many more that make the Hudson, a team effort by Ian Schrager and Philippe Starck, so special. While some complain its thousand rooms are too small, others argue that its artistic public spaces, haute yacht-like guest rooms (dark African wood paneling; modern, white-tiled bathrooms; stainless steel tables), and reasonable rates more

than make up for the fact that you can't do a proper cartwheel next to the bed. By day, sunbathe on the Sky Terrace or take in the cool charms of its indoor-outdoor private park; by night, mingle underneath the Hudson Bar's ceiling fresco by painter Francesco Clemente. Fashionable flocks chat over modernized comfort food at Jeffrey Chodorow's Hudson Cafeteria, a candlelit, Viking-esque dining hall with communal wood table and stained-glass windows. The staff certainly isn't ugly, and they know what they're doing, too.

Style 7, Atmosphere 8, Location 8

Jumeirah Essex House, 160 Central Park South (7th), Midtown West

Tel: 212 247 0300 www.jumeirahessexhouse.com
Rates: $319–1,229

Formerly the Westin Essex House, this landmark Art Deco luxury property on Central Park South recently changed ownership and underwent a $70

million refurbishment, endowing its grand lobby and 515 rooms and suites with top-tier modern flourishes that blend seamlessly with its upper-crust interior design. Rooms come with king or queen beds and are done up in rich reds and gold, with honey wood cabinetry and red-leather framed mirrors, while flat-screen TVs and modern gadgets give it some contemporary credibility. Built in 1931, this classic property has been deluxe from the very start, yet its latest incarnation is appealing to both the younger set that loves its location and longtime fans that are continually awed by its grandeur. Grab afternoon tea in its classic

Lobby Lounge, or reserve at the Restaurant at the Essex House for fine Mediterranean-New American fare.

Style 8, Atmosphere 7, Location 9

The Library Hotel, 299 Madison Avenue (E 41st St), Midtown East

Tel: 212 983 4500   www.libraryhotel.com

Rates: $249–609

For the booksmart traveler, there's no better choice of hotel than this boutique concept in a landmark brownstone building around the corner from Grand Central Station, with its storybook opulence and reverence for the written word. Each of its 10 floors is dedicated to a category of the Dewey Decimal system, and each of its 60 rooms boasts a theme – think categories like Economics, Fairy Tales, and Love. Elegantly appointed with quilted headboards, deluxe bedding,  Deco furniture, and healthy plants, rooms offer guests art and books that relate to its appointed topic. Exclusive-feeling and clubby, the Library contains over 6,000 carefully selected volumes (if those are not enough, the New York Public Library and the Pierpont Morgan Library are a quick stroll away). Making the experience all the more satisfying are the complimentary deluxe breakfast buffet, wine and cheese each evening, in-room Belgian chocolates, and afternoon snacks in the transporting second-floor reading room.

Style 8, Atmosphere 8, Location 7

Loews Regency Hotel, 540 Park Avenue (E 61st St), Upper East Side
Tel: 212 759 4100   www.loewshotels.com
Rates: $509–1,549

Few hostelries conjure up a snappier, ritzier vibe than the Regency, home to the city's most acclaimed cabaret venue and hotel of choice to countless fancy folks, including screen stars and royalty. Every detail within the 353

sunny guest rooms, 75 suites, and 11 specialty suites has been meticulously considered, from oversized work stations with ergonomic chairs to top-of-the-line electronics (including flat-screen TVs) and king-sized beds with top-tier linens and plenty of luxurious throw pillows. Great care has been taken to select the finest bath towel and robes, and all-natural toiletries are provided by Bloom. Suites feature nice touches such as wood parquet entrances and chic vanities. Downstairs, titans of industry hold meetings at classy breakfast/lunch spot 540 Park, while the Library is a fantastic, banquette-lined lounge filled with books and international newspapers. All the while, Feinstein's at the Regency presents world-class cabaret performers and classic American fare.

Style 9, Atmosphere 8, Location 8

The London NYC, 151 West 54th Street (6th Ave), Upper West Side
Tel: 866 690 2029   www.thelondonnyc.com
Rates: $99–1,500

A formidable new contender in the high-end hotel game, this superbly conceived, 562-suite hotel – formerly the RIGHA Royal Hotel – brings together experts of design, service, gastronomy, and fitness to create a ritzy retreat you'd gladly move right into. Billed as the Manhattan pied-à-terre, the London's pervasive sense of cool was orchestrated by interior design stand-out David Collins, who bestowed each room with limed oak parquet floors and custom designed the furniture, including rocking chairs and embossed-leather desks. (There is a bedchamber and a parlor space in each suite.) King-sized beds are topped with Fili D'Oro linens, and bathrooms were designed by bath company Waterworks – complete with rain showerheads, mosaic tiles, and the company's signature apothecary products. Renowned concierge service Quintessentially does a superb job to tackle guests' needs and desires. On the fourth floor, the London NYC Club is an urbanized fitness oasis, complete with state-of-the-art conditioning gear and a luxurious spa. And perhaps most impressive (because it certainly has been buzzworthy) is the arrival of superstar Brit chef Gordon Ramsay, who creates adventurous fare at his eponymous, tiny restaurant while overseeing the marvelous small plates at the London Bar and the hotel's room service menu.

Style 8, Atmosphere 8, Location 8

The Mandarin Oriental New York, 80 Columbus Circle (W 60th St), Upper West Side

Tel: 212 805 8800, 866 801 8880 www.mandarinoriental.com
Rates: $745–1,900

The Mandarin Oriental family of hotels has long been known as the standard-bearer of peaceful, Asian-inspired luxury, and this outpost – located atop the Time Warner Center is no exception. Within its 202 standard rooms and 46 suites, guests marvel at floor-to-ceiling views of the Hudson River or Central Park and the metropolis beyond it. Sweeping floor plans

feature unparalleled entertainment technology, black enamel furniture accented with Asian flourishes, sumptuous beds outfitted with Fili D'Oro linens, and fully stocked bars. Bathrooms are fitted with marble tubs (which have their own flat-screen TVs) as well as separate showers, and are stocked with Aromatherapy Associates bath products. The 14,500 square foot spa very well may be the best in the city, offering a vast selection of treatments that combine Eastern and Western techniques. Its superior fitness center features a 75-foot indoor lap pool that looks out onto the Hudson. Acclaimed French-Japanese fusion restaurant Asiate draws top-city foodies, while its come-as-you-are Lobby Lounge and ritzy cocktail spot MObar serve up potent potables. As would be expected, the staff round out the experience with their competence and friendliness.

Style 10, Atmosphere 9, Location 9

The Mansfield Hotel, 12 West 44th Street (5th), Midtown
Tel: 212 277 8700, 800 255 5167 www.mansfieldhotel.com
Rates: $239–560

A serene escape conjuring turn-of-last-century grandeur, this landmark building dating back to 1903 has been lovingly preserved and outfitted with top contemporary luxuries (that don't intrude on the romantic, refined feel of the space). The M Bar off the lobby is great for stealing away moments with a paramour, with its private seating areas, domed skylight, mahogany

bookshelves, and menu of light bites and specialty cocktails. Meanwhile, the Club Room is a magical Beaux Arts library, complete with a grand fireplace, table games, and a London phone booth room (ideal for carrying out breathy conversations). Upstairs, its 126 handsomely appointed rooms include several suite options and boast elegant Deco furniture, ebony-stained hardwood floors, 300 count linens, pillow-top mattresses, iHome alarm clock radios for the iPod, and flat-panel LCD TVs. Bathrooms are stocked up with Aveda products. If you feel you've been luxuriating too long, get motivated and hit the fitness center, complete with a yoga loft.

Style 8, Atmosphere 8, Location 7

The Maritime Hotel, 363 West 16th Street (9th), Meatpacking District

Tel: 212 242 4300 www.themaritimehotel.com
Rates: $315–1,400

The cruise ship theme that pulls together this handsome hostelry on the Chelsea/Meatpacking District border might be a bit much for more buttoned-up, gimmick-resistant travelers. But its attentive staff, fine amenities (500 count sheets, flat-screen television, bath products by C.O. Bigelow), and prime location more than satisfy the chic set that return to it time and again. Although the Maritime is often overshadowed by its pricier boutique neighbor The Gansevoort, weary travelers will most likely find it gracious, welcoming, and full of charms – think: porthole windows; the al fresco, South Beach-style event space Cabanas; the striking Hiro Ballroom, plucked

from the imagination of a kung-fu movie's set designer; and two fine dining establishments – the fashionable rustic Italian La Bottega and chef Tadashi Ono's glitzy Matsuri.

Style 8, Atmosphere 8, Location 9

The Mercer Hotel, 147 Mercer Street (Prince), Soho
Tel: 212 966 6060 www.mercerhotel.com
Rates: $495–1,500

There's much to love about this elegant, 75-room boutique beauty, which has played host to everybody who's anybody at one time or another. A natural choice for sophisticates whose social sensibilities, fashionable work, or shopping addictions lead them to Soho, the Mercer – sister property to LA's legendary Chateau Marmont – is housed in a landmark Romanesque

revival building on one of the neighborhood's most stylish corners. Staffed primarily with capable model types, the hotel provides end-of-the-earth service and offers a wide range of services – packing and unpacking, personal training, chauffeurs, overnight shoe shines, same-day laundry, and excellent anytime concierge. You even get your own local cell phone to use. Rooms were designed by interiors legend Christian Liaigre, who kept things elegant, simple, and cushy – dark wood dining furniture and floors, plush seating, handsome king-sized beds with 400-thread-count sheets, and soothing bathrooms with sexy marble soaking tubs and a stock of FACE Stockholm bath products. All the while, fashion and media types buzz in, out of, and around Jean Georges Vongericthen's celebrated French-American eatery (The Mercer) Kitchen.

Style 8, Atmosphere 9, Location 9

Morgans Hotel, 237 Madison Avenue (E 36th St), Murray Hill
Tel: 212 686 0300 www.morganshotel.com
Rates: $300–500

Handsome, intimate, and classic, with up-to-the-minute flourishes, the Morgans – the namesake of one of America's top boutique hotel chains –

hits all its marks, with a super-chic lobby (complete with a 3D marble floor and deluxe leather club chairs), perennially packed Asian fusion eatery Asia de Cuba, hotspot the Morgans Bar, and beautifully conceived interiors by Andree Putman. Opened in 1985, it was a trailblazer in the boutique genre of hotels, and continues to lure in smart travelers with its dramatic visuals and superb service. Each of its 113 guest rooms features, among its many special touches, a Robert Mapplethorpe photograph – not to mention ultrasuede banquettes, cushy bedding, top electronics, and a gorgeous black-and-white tiled bathroom stocked with Aqua products. (Save time for an extra-long bath.)

Style 8, Atmosphere 8, Location 7

Le Parker Meridien, 118 West 57th Street (6th), Upper West Side
Tel: 212 245 5000 www.parkermeridien.com
Rates: $250–1,500

For a stylish stay that doesn't skimp on fun or polish, this classic, 731-room property hits its marks from the lobby (atrium and painted columns includ-

ed) to the Presidential Suite. Everything is deliberate and deluxe – from its elevators featuring classic TV loops to the modern flourishes of its guest rooms and suites. There's an exceptional concierge service called "New York Smart Aleck" that provides plenty of insider tips and access for visitors. Three very different restaurants – breakfast haven Norma's, the greasy spoon Burger Joint (see Snack), and posh French bistro Seppi's – tend to your deepest gastronomic desires. Its expansive fitness center, Gravity, offers an impressive rooftop pool, racquetball and basketball courts, and top-of-the-line conditioning equipment. Bedrooms come with high concept plank beds, Aeron chairs, expansive workstations, spacious showers, and all the electronics you'll need.

Style 8, Atmosphere 8, Location 9

The Peninsula, 700 Fifth Avenue (55th St), Upper East Side
Tel: 212 956 2888   www.peninsula.com
Rates: $625–2,800

Embodying a singular sense of luxury, this luscious Midtown boutique hotel draws a cultivated clientele that craves ease and elegance over hard-partying or overdone stuffiness. Residing in a landmark 1905 Beaux Arts building – it was formerly the Gotham Hotel – the Peninsula greets newcomers with its

sweeping, foliage and trompe l'oeil bedecked lobby with dual staircases, while attentive desk staffers set a soothing mood while checking you in. Done up in beiges, golds, and splashes of color, and

accented by Deco photos and prints, each guest room is individually decorated and presents an opulent mix of old-school charm and newfangled technology. A bedside control panel allows you to adjust music, lighting, and temperature with ease, and there are flat-screen TVs and phones by the bathtubs. There are several sleek spots to make merry – from the Pen-Top & Terrace rooftop bar, with its stupendous skyline views, to Fives, the lobby's lovely Mediterranean restaurant. The Bar at Fives features live piano, light bites, and specialty Martinis. If you've got energy to burn, the tri-level spa and gym – complete with a swimming pool – will get you toned up in style.

Style 9, Atmosphere 8, Location 8

The Pierre New York, 2 East 61st St (5th), Upper East Side
Tel: 212 838 8000   www.tajhotels.com
Rates: $720–4,900

A decadent, deluxe stay, the Pierre – taking up an entire block across from
Central Park – spares no expense to make guests feel privileged. Its 149
rooms, 40 suites, and 12 grand suites are decked out to dramatic proportions; it was designed to emulate the Palace of Versailles, and one could easily see Marie Antoinette holding court within its dark wood-accented confines. Formerly a Four Seasons property, now owned by Indian luxury chain
Taj, the Pierre features a knowledgeable concierge and multilingual staff; two
salons (Dominique on the first floor, Rene on the fourth); a 1,600-square-
foot fitness center; luxurious spa services performed in private rooms; and
several upper-crust dining options. Breakfast, lunch, and the Pierre's fabled
English afternoon tea take place in the dazzling Rotunda, while Café Pierre is
a haute contemporary French eatery with a 10,000 bottle wine cellar. The
Café Pierre Bar is great for hors d'oeuvres, snacks, cocktails, and wines by
the glass.

Style 9, Atmosphere 9, Location 9

Plaza Athénée, 37 East 64th Street (Madison), Upper East Side

Tel: 212 734 9100 www.plaza-athenee.com
Rates: $695–5,600

We could all use a little Parisian glamour from time to time, and this grand
Upper East Side beauty – the sister property to the famed Parisian Plaza
Athénée – delivers it in spades. Guests are greeted by bright red awnings
and dapper doormen, and led inside to a ritzy tiled, fresco-lined lobby.
Superb desk help and bellmen are competent and warm, and a 24-hour

"clefs d'or" concierge service is extremely cosseting. Once inside one of the 114 guest rooms or 35 suites — a handful with indoor atriums, dining rooms,

and balconies peering out onto Fifth Avenue — you'll find elegant furnishings done up in European fabrics and floor plans unique to each room. Roomy — and pet-friendly — each guest room features a dining area, a sizable writing desk, fine Belgian linens, and subtle modern amenities that blend in seamlessly with the upper crust décor. Other touches include shoe shines in the lobby, afternoon tea and coffee served between 5.30 and 7pm, the swank Moroccan-themed lounge called Bar Seine, and fine French restaurant Arabelle.

Style 9, Atmosphere 8, Location 9

The Ritz Carlton New York, 50 Central Park South (6th), Midtown West
Tel: 212 308 9100   www.ritzcarlton.com
Rates: $575–15,000

Any Ritz is going to dazzle you… but this one, on one of the cushiest blocks in Manhattan, is pure, old-school luxury. Views of Central Park, right across the street, are delicious (if you shell out for one), and service is both abundant and hard to argue with. The 260 guest rooms and 49 suites conjure the ritzy glamour of an Upper East Side home, with sumptuous couches, deluxe Bang & Olufsen stereos, and grand comfy beds topped by 400-thread-count linens. The bathrooms offer both a marble tub and a stand-up shower, and feature exclusive Frederic Fekkai bath products. For the weary

travelers among us, renowned spa La Priarie is on-site and works wonders
on overtaxed minds and bodies. Meanwhile, chef Laurent Tourondel expands
the BLT brand with his latest offering, BLT Market – a stunning, season-
driven eatery with a cloistered al fresco area.

Style 9, Atmosphere 8, Location 9

The Royalton, 44 West 44th Street (5th), Midtown West
Tel: 212 869 4400 www.royaltonhotel.com
Rates: $229–750

One of the first – and still one
of the best – boutique hotels
in Manhattan, this swanky,
Philippe Starck-designed property from the Morgans Hotel
Group (also owners of Miami's
Delano and New York's
Hudson and Morgans hotels)
sets the standard for the lobby
schmoozing and boundary-
pushing décor. The brainchild of
Ian Schrager and the late Steve
Rubell (the team behind Studio
54), the Royalton was built to
encourage cool crowds to
commingle, the Philippe Starck-

designed lobby teases the eye with a seemingly endless blue carpet – the length of the entire block – and low lighting sets a sexy tone. The curved velvet banquettes of its restaurant 44 have long drawn tastemakers and chi-chi types, while the tiny Round Bar is the picture of cool with its rounded, tufted leather walls with built-in banquettes. There is also the Library Table – a 20-foot marble table in the lobby stocked with a slick collection of books. It's not all about the socializing, though… the 169 oversized rooms and suites have custom Starck-designed furniture, banquette seating along the width of the rooms, 300-thread-count Egyptian sheets, and slate bathrooms with stainless steel fixtures – plus, some rooms have fireplaces and five-foot-round two-person tubs.

Style 8, Atmosphere 8, Location 8

St. Regis, 2 East 55th Street (5th), Midtown East
Tel: 212 753 4500 www.stregis.com
Rates: $600–1,500

For a decadent dose of old New York, you can't do much better than this Beaux Arts masterpiece, built in 1904 by John Jacob Astor as a ritzy retreat

for his most manorly international friends. Having recently undergone an extensive, $100 million facelift, the Reege is a thoroughly modern gal these days, despite its century-old pedigree, and delivers guests in any of its spacious 182 guest rooms or 72 suites a satisfying combination of hidden modernity and well-maintained, old New York aplomb. For something truly unique, go for one of the designer suites, each individually themed and done up to the nines. An unparalleled butler service will make you feel like a turn-of-the-century tycoon yourself, while tea in the gilded Astor Court is a study in a buttoned-up treat. Meanwhile, the King Cole Bar houses Maxfield Parish's mural of Old King Cole, who still lords over this mainstay of refined tippling.

Style 9, Atmosphere 8, Location 8

Soho Grand, 310 West Broadway (Canal), Soho
Tel: 212 965 3000 www.sohogrand.com
Rates: $424–800

Reserve for the location, stay for the sex appeal at this 363-room bastion of earth-toned comfort, just a spiked-heeled stroll away from all the boutique shopping your heart could desire. The sister property of the nearby Tribeca Grand, this hip little hotel is a nice embodiment of privileged Soho style from the past two decades. Designed by interior designer William Sofield in the mid-1990s, Soho Grand features a suspended glass bottle staircase in

the entryway that leads to the lobby and the Grand Bar & Lounge – decked out with comfy couches, populated by posh folk, and energized by the sound of top DJs. The Gallery is a second, more avant-garde dining room, and the Yard opens up in the summer months for al fresco noshing. The neutral-toned guest rooms feature Frette linens, Malin + Goetz bath products, flat-screen TVs, and digital cable.

Style 8, Atmosphere 8, Location 8

Soho House New York, 29–35 Ninth Avenue (W 14th St), Meatpacking District

Tel: 212 627 9800 www.sohohouseny.com
Rates: $495–1,350

Once a warehouse on a busy Meatpacking District street, the Soho House New York has become a bastion of British panache and insider decadence. The sister property of London's famous Soho House, where giants of the

journalism world and the bold-faced set mix and mingle away from the maddening crowds, New York's Soho House is first and foremost a private club, with a sexy rooftop pool deck, a hopping private restaurant that ushers in the who's-who nightly, a classic game room, private party spots, and a bar room that's perfect for high-powered flirtation across the arm of its 39-foot Chesterfield sofa. A reservation at one of the House's 24 marvelous, loft-style rooms is your ticket in, although the rooms are so chic that you might be hesitant to venture beyond your front door. Expect: brick walls, exposed wood beams, chandeliers, top-tier bedding, the

latest in personal entertainment technology, and bath products from Cowshed (the famed British spa, which has an outpost on the property). All this, plus sublime location and insider access: sounds good, no?

Style 9, Atmosphere 9, Location 9

Tribeca Grand, 2 Avenue of the Americas (White), Tribeca

Tel: 212 519 6600 www.tribecagrand.com
Rates: $424–1,050

Having packed in boldfaced crowds since 2000, this thoroughly urban, 203-room hideaway trades on its cool factor in every way possible—from its selection of deluxe, up-to-the-minute amenities to the eye-candy staff. Housed in a triangular building at the base of Sixth Avenue, the lobby opens onto a grand, industrial-chic atrium that spans eight floors, and lets in plenty

of opaque light. The ritzy Church Lounge serves up satisfying global fare and draws a slinky crowd once the sun goes down. Guest rooms are fully wired and boast Bose sound systems, bath products from luxury apothecary We Live Like This, and special request features such as iPod sound docks or even your own pet goldfish.

Style 8, Atmosphere 8, Location 8

Trump International Hotel and Tower, 1 Central Park West (Columbus Circle), Upper West Side
Tel: 212 299 1000; 888 44 TRUMP www.trumpintl.com
Rates: $725–3,000

In true Trump style, this glitzy, 52-story tower is a true tycoon's hotel, with a showy bronze exterior, spacious rooms (three-quarters of which are actually suites), spectacular views of Central Park and the city skyline, and a personalized staffer who is ready at your beck and call and will remain versed in your tastes for future visits. Jean-Georges, one of the city's most decadent dining experiences, is located here, so that's a big plus. Deluxe rooms feature fully equipped kitchens, crystal and china, deluxe entertainment centers, 300-count Italian linens, fresh flowers – and even a telescope. The all-marble

bathrooms are well stocked with Forest Essentials products and grooming gear, and feature Jacuzzi tubs. It's not the subtlest hotel in town, but it certainly is deluxe.

Style 8, Atmosphere 7, Location 9

The W Union Square, 201 Park Avenue South (E 17th St), Flatiron/Gramercy Park
Tel: 212 253 9119 www.whotels.com
Rates: $669–3,500

Out of all the "W"s in the city, of which there are five, this beacon – the 1911 Guardian Life building situated at the Northeast corner of 17th Street and Park Avenue South – combines the chic environs and modernist amenities of the chain with a very desirable downtown address, not to mention

the largest room size of all of the NYC properties. With easy access to furniture shopping in Flatiron District, the green market of Union Square across the street, the action of Greenwich Village, and a straight-shot taxi ride to Midtown East, W Union Square draws a monied, young-spirited clientele. Spa and fitness services are available, and pets are welcome. The open Living Room lounge is prime people-watching territory; chef Todd English's Olive's restaurant delivers very nice wood-oven Mediterranean fare; and Rande Gerber's Underbar is a candlelit, subterranean *boîte* ideally suited for seducing your spouse or... whoever.

Style 8, Atmosphere 8, Location 9

Waldorf Astoria, 301 Park Avenue, Midtown East
Tel: 212 355 3000 www.hilton.com
Rates: $319–10,000

One of the truly great New York luxury hotels, the sprawling Waldorf —

now owned by Hilton — is steeped in tradition, and a Deco enthusiast's dream. Despite a longstanding epidemic of tourist foot traffic, the lobby remains grand and transporting, and several marvelous restaurants and lounges are on-site. Its 1,300 rooms vary in size and décor, but each promises to be lavishly (and traditionally) decorated, with work desks, marble bathrooms (some with tubs; do check), plush beds with triple-sheeting, and fresh flowers. The lobby's handsome all-day eatery, Peacock Alley, is delightful for brunch, while Oscar's serves up fine

American brasserie fare. Inagiku is a dramatic Japanese offering, though be sure to grab a perfectly prepared rib-eye at the renowned Bull & Bear steakhouse. At the end of the evening, stop into throwback bar Sir Harry's for a top-shelf nightcap.

Style 8, Atmosphere 8, Location 7

eat...

Perhaps the most daunting task of this book was trying to pare down the list of restaurants worthy of attention while visiting New York. Thousands of them exist, and so many of them are marvelous. There are the celebrity chefs and their gleeful gastronomic destinations; the hidden little joints that use their locations and real estate to create singular experiences that can't be replicated; the old standbys that hit their marks every time; the newest and most buzzed about efforts that might just be a flash in the pan; and diverse offerings from every corner of the globe – and, not only do we advocate 'ethnic adventuring', we adore the term 'ethnic adventuring'.

What we tried to do was give you a range of cuisines, neighborhoods, price points, and vibes that have one vital thing in common – they, in one way or another, embody what's exciting about the New York food scene. You won't find Daniel Boulud's Daniel, David Bouley's Danube, Mario Batali's Babbo, or the eponymous restaurant of Jean-Georges Vongerichten. Neither will you find the Water Club, the Spice Market, or *Vanity Fair* editor Graydon Carter's intimidatingly popular incarnation of the Waverly Inn. Why? These places (a) don't need the publicity and (b) have been reviewed in plenty of other places.

The ones you will find were chosen in the spirit of variety. If nothing tickles your fancy, ask your concierge or local friends for a recommendation. Most New Yorker's love to share their favorite eateries, and fancy themselves amateur critics. (right, Gin Lane)

In keeping with the 'hedonism' umbrella of this

guidebook, we'd like to assure you that wining and dining with abandon are possible in every neighborhood and in any variation you can think of. We went to lengths to select a healthy assortment of eateries, but don't be nervous to look beyond our pages – we won't be offended. You can swim through the extensive wine offerings of Cru or Veritas, or plan several consecutive days' worth of fine eating on East 12th Street with knockout steakhouse the Strip House, master chef Alfred Portale's Gotham Bar & Grill, and killer comfort food spot Stand. Sushi star Nobu Matsuhisu reigns supreme with Nobu and Nobu Next Door in Tribeca, while chef extraordinaire Eric Ripert re-earns his four-star reputation nightly at Le Bernardin on West 51st Street. Rumor has it that Alain Ducasse is reopening his dynamic eponymous restaurant at the St. Regis hotel (hooray!); meanwhile the Lever House on Park and 53rd continues to draw heavy hitters with its cool, podlike architecture and dynamic cuisine. Feeling like a czar? Treat yourself to the Russian Tea Room, Firebird, or Petrossian. Classic New York pizza? Lombardi's on Spring Street, John's on Bleecker, or Arturo's on Houston and Thompson Street. We like Artisanal for high-end fondue, and either Estiatorio Milos in Midtown West or Parea in the Flatiron District for Greek. We could really do this all day, so let's stop here. (above, Public)

Oh, one other thing: a restaurant reviewer's word is not law. Just because we say a tacqueria is divine or a bistro's chicken is dry or a concierge is snooty does not mean you'll feel the same way. Come to eat with an open mind and an empty stomach. The prices we give are for the cost of two courses and half a bottle of wine for one.

Top 10 restaurants in New York:
1. Gramercy Tavern
2. WD–50
3. Chanterelle
4. Del Posto
5. Degustation
6. Perry Street
7. Applewood
8. Telepan
9. Momofoku Ssam Bar
10. BLT Steak

Top 5 restaurants for food:
1. WD–50
2. Gramercy Tavern
3. Chanterelle
4. Degustation
5. Blue Ribbon

Top 5 restaurants for service:
1. Chanterelle
2. Applewood
3. Gramercy Tavern
4. Del Posto
5. Perry Street

Top 5 restaurants for atmosphere:
1. Gramercy Tavern
2. 5 Ninth
3. Freeman's
4. The Harrison
5. Fiamma

5 Ninth, 5 Ninth Avenue, Meatpacking District

Tel: 212 929 9460 www.5ninth.com

Open: noon–11pm Mon–Fri; 11am–12.30am Sat/Sun

American/Asian

Providing a pretty, placid escape from the scene-y absurdity of the
Meatpacking District, this three-story townhouse at the convergence of the
neighborhood's swanky cobblestone streets is the winning creation of
chef/co-owner Zac Pelaccio, a young culinary star who cut his teeth at the
dearly departed Chickenbone Café in Williamsburg, Brooklyn. Known for its

lack of outdoor signage (just a bronze "5" on the weathered door), its
seductively simple wooden interiors, its handsome glowing bar (not to mention barkeeps), its communal lounging floor, and the darling, color-dotted
backyard garden, 5 Ninth is a place where chic and discerning diners can
amble up to the bar for stellar signature cocktails (the gin, lime, and ginger
ale Florodora is lifted by a raspberry shot; Cameron's Kick blends Scotch
and Irish whiskies with lemon juice and almond syrup) or a nice glass of
Sancerre between spending a delightful hour or two in Pelaccio's able hands.
Known for his sophisticated global style – culled undoubtedly from years at
French Laundry and Daniel – Pelaccio plies diners with lovingly adorned
lobster and scallops, braises and steams a mean pork shoulder, fries up a
marvelous chili-bedecked red snapper, and turns out one of the finest
brunches in town.

Food 8, Service 7, Atmosphere 9

Alta, 64 West 10th Street (5th), West Village

Tel: 212 505 7777 www.altarestaurant.com
Open: daily, 5.30–11pm (1am Fri/Sat, 10.30pm Sun) $52
International Tapas

It's easy to fall in love with everything at this handsome, hacienda-style spot,
from the plant-lined patio entrance (just west of Fifth Avenue) to the haute-

rustic, honey-lit dining
areas (including a bi-level
room at the rear) and its
cleverly rendered small
plates – the highest-brow
tapas – complemented by
a nice, knowing selection
of Mediterranean wines,
including a great group of
Spanish whites.
Neighborhood regulars
are often found sidling up
to the long wooden bar
for their precious bites of
Moroccan spiced cashews,
lamb meatballs in brown
butter *lebne*, crabmeat
cannelloni with crème

fraiche, or pork tenderloin confit, although for a special evening we suggest
you try for a bird's eye table… There aren't many that look out over the
subterranean space, but if you score one it's a special view to savor.

Food 8, Service 8, Atmosphere 8

Antique Garage, 41 Mercer Street (Grand), Soho

Tel: 212 219 1019 www.antiquegaragesoho.com
Open: daily, noon–11pm (midnight Fri/Sat) $58
Mediterranean

One of the more charming, attitude-free eateries in Soho, the Antique
Garage – a former auto garage now decorated entirely in for-sale antiques –
rides high on its charms yet never lets diners down when it comes to well-

conceived, flavorful mezze plates from chef/owner Utku Cinel. Cinel manipulates his fresh, pan-Mediterranean ingredients with an alchemic flair – he cites French, Italian, and Turkish influences as well as modernized Ottoman

cuisine – and serves his punchy, colorful offerings in handsome vintage dishware. Some favorites: spicy shrimp sautéed in butter with Roma tomatoes and hot peppers, grilled Turkish-spiced lamb and beef meatballs, and the eye-pleasing Shepherd salad with its chunky chopped tomatoes, cucumbers, and green peppers. A sidewalk seat during the summer months, when the garage door lifts onto the street, is bliss.

Food 8, Service 7, Atmosphere 7

Apizz, 217 Eldridge Street (Stanton), Lower East Side
Tel: 212 253 9199   www.apizz.com
Open: 6–11pm. Closed Sundays. $60
Italian

Stepping out of the cab, you may look around and ask, "Is this the right place?" Yes, indeed, it is – and its location, on a less savory Lower East Side street than, say, WD-50, makes it all the more appealing as your enter into its warm, cozy confines to find a lush dining room, smiling hosts, and a satisfying menu conceived and regularly altered by affable chef/owner John LaFemina. A grand hearth looms large, as do its potent fragrances, holding the room in a warm haze as skilled waiters in black tend to your needs with casual aplomb. LaFemina – a former diamond merchant who cut his teeth in the NYC restaurant scene as a co-owner at Nolita's Peasant, pours his creativity into Apizz's menu, from flavor-packed thin-crust pizzas and award-

winning meatballs to well-executed al dente pastas (such as wild boar ragu lasagna) and rosemary-lifted whole roasted fish of the day. Its wine menu is small but spot on.

Food 8, Service 8, Atmosphere 7

Applewood, 501 11th Street (7th), Park Slope, Brooklyn

Tel: 718 768 2044 www.applewoodny.com
Open: 5–11pm Tues–Sat; 10am–3pm Sun $53
American

Everything about this comforting Park Slope eatery feels right. It is on a (requisite) bucolic tree-lined block of this peaceful, family-fueled neighborhood. The owners, David and Laura Shea, run a meticulous ship and serve stand-out fare created from "slow food" ingredients – veggies from independent farms, hormone and antibiotic free, etc. Their family unit is a vital

yet unobtrusive element in the restaurant's success; their relationships with local farmers ensure that they deliver spectacular quality. David's daily-changing menu celebrates each moment of the year – anything from sautéed Maine lobster risotto to pan-roasted Vermont lamb loin or Long Island duck breast. Brunch is a pleasure, and if the weather permits, Seventh Avenue is a grand place to shop and walk off the stellar meal.

Food 9, Service 9, Atmosphere 9

Balthazar, 80 Spring Street (Crosby), Soho
Tel: 212 965 1414 www.balthazarny.com
Open: daily, 7.30am (8am Sat/Sun)–1am (2am Fri/Sat, midnight Sun) $65
French

Come looking delicious to this mainstay of downtown hobnobbery and good gastronomy; the first feather in prolific restaurateur Keith McNally's cap. Popular since its opening in 1997, there is rarely a dull moment within this wonderful looking mirrored bistro as crisply attired waiters and bus-boys buzz between the tiny tables and red leather banquettes packed with

PR gals schmoozing editors, curious Soho passers-by, and nostalgic foodies. (When McNally builds something, the hip crowds will come; his is the mind behind the Odeon, Lucky Strike, the dearly departed Café Luxembourg, and Lower East Side power scene Schiller's Liquor Bar.) A well-executed classic cocktail at the zinc bar provides a nice salve from being scrutinized by fel-low patrons, while classic bistro fare and satisfying house specials – escar-gots, steak au poivre, and duck confit as well as cider-braised pork hock and grilled chicken Paillard – still arrive well executed after all these years.

Food 8, Service 7, Atmosphere 8

Le Bilboquet, 25 East 63rd St (Madison), Upper East Side

Tel: 212 751 3036

Open: daily, noon–11pm

$78

French

While socialites and trust-funders find themselves quite at home at this stylish, cramped, haute bistro – located in the thick of other scene-y Upper East Side French spots such as La Goulue, Demarchelier, Aureole, and Le

Charlot – you'll get along like an insider once seated at one of the comfy blue banquettes, bopping to the clubby soundtrack and sampling such classics as melt-away beef carpaccio, tuna tartare, and niçoise salad. But there's much more than old stand-bys... duck Magret is kissed with flavorful mango chutney; tender chicken is blackened with bursting Cajun spices. Making your evening all the more stimulating are some of the more attractive waiters in town: knowledgeable, flirtatious, skilled in tight quarters.

Food 8, Service 6, Atmosphere 7

BLT Steak, 106 East 57th Street (Park Ave), Midtown East

Tel: 212 752 7470

Open: 11.45am–2.30pm, 5.30–11pm (11.30pm Fri/Sat). Closed Sundays.

Steakhouse

$100

Chef Laurent Tourondel – whose departed Cello on the Upper East Side announced him to New York food snobs – has spent the last few years re-proving his aptitude for pleasing big-spending, big city appetites, with Chelsea's BLT Fish; the Gramercy Park chophouse BLT Prime; and BLT

Steak, the first spot of the 2000s, which has earned him the greatest culinary recognition and laid his claim to the initials BLT (Bistro Laurent Tourondel). As much a feast for the eyes as for the palate, the space is a sexy escape from Midtown, with a plush lounge anchored by a lengthy zinc bar. Its main dining room, however, is a hive of activity; a striking stage for Tourondel's brand of dining with abandon. American Kobe skirt steak is marinated in fragrant herbs; the veal chop is imposing and incredibly tender; spiced swordfish is a marvelous alternative to the red meat. Sides such as onion rings and potato gratin are lifted to new heights, while sauces such as the three mustard, classic béarnaise, or horseradish make sure all senses are humming by the time the check comes.

Food 9, Service 8, Atmosphere 8

Blue Ribbon, 97 Sullivan Street (Spring), Soho
Tel: 212 274 0404   www.blueribbonrestaurants.com
Open: daily, 4pm–4am $60
Modern American

There are few greater compliments for a restaurant than maintaining a following of the top critics, off-duty chefs, and discriminating diners night after night – and late into the night, at that. (Dinner is served until 4am every night; no reservations for parties of four or under… even you.) This eclectic, market-driven new American spot from chefs/owners Bruce and Eric Bromberg subscribe to no formula or ethos other than that the ingredients should sing, that variety is the spice of life, and that everything – caviar, barbecued ribs, *matzoh* ball soup, fried chicken with mashed potatoes, paella,

sweetbreads – is fair game. Of course, there are mainstays such as the raw bar – arguably the best in the city – and the understated decadence of the chocolate Bruno dessert. Do expect to contend with lines filled with self-important folks, and a legendary volume issue (your ears may ring the next morning). But it's worth it, otherwise none of you would be there.

Food 9, Service 7, Atmosphere 7

Bouillabaisse 126, 126 Union Street, Red Hook, Brooklyn
Tel: 718 855 4405   www.bouillabaisse126.com
Open: 5–10pm (10.30pm Fri/Sat). Closed Wednesdays. $50
French

To get to Bouillabaisse 126, it's a bit of a stretch of the legs from the F train subway (to Carroll Street), so perhaps just take a cab to Union Street and

Columbia, where Yugoslavian chef Neil Ganic oversees a manly room – wood slab tables, menus scrawled on slate that are lugged around by eccentric European waiters, a decidedly intentional lack of decoration that leaves plenty of focus on the flavors that unfold. The flavorful fish stew for which the eatery is named is always worth ordering, as are the mussels Dijonaise, a crab cake to write home about, and the satisfying rack of lamb with Provençal herbs. There's a decent selection of wines, plus Mondays (and only Mondays) feature a BYOB service with no corkage fee.

Food 8, Service 8, Atmosphere 7

Bread, 20 Spring Street (Elizabeth), Nolita
Tel: 212 334 1015
Open: daily, 9.30am–midnight (1am Thurs–Sat) $30
Italian

The vibe at Bread – only occasionally disrupted by an overdose of demanding weekend night crowds – is an encapsulation of the elements that make its neighborhood, Nolita, so chic and satisfying. In its open kitchen, an able chef staff creates remarkable Italian sandwiches using fine, fresh ingredients

and heavenly bread from Balthazar Bakery, Keith McNally's neighboring boulangerie. The simple flickering of candles sets off the scene – eye-catching local artists' wares hung on the white walls; metallic tables, chairs, and bar; fetching waiters who never seem to tire despite the maddening crowds. Much has been made of the organic tomato soup, nicely complementing panini such as Italian tuna with lemon dressing or any of its can't-fail combinations of Italian meats and cheeses. It's a simple, straightforward concept… and everyone wants a piece.

Food 7, Service 7, Atmosphere 7

Café Habana, 17 Prince Street (Elizabeth), Nolita
Tel: 212 625 2002   www.ecoeatery.com
Open: daily, 9am–midnight $38
Latin American

While the hefty crowds and cooler-than-thou attitude of some of the clientele might inspire hot-headedness, this much-loved dive with its throwback chrome exterior and pleasantly efficient waitstaff will easily win you over once you've waited your turn and settled into a tiny booth. Cheap, tasty, and true to its Mexican and Cuban roots (it is family-run and modeled after the original Café Habana in Mexico City), Habana satiates a pretty gathering of well-heeled boutique shoppers and devoted locals, offering tempting takes on Cuban pork sandwiches, cheese-dusted Mexican grilled corn, and marinated skirt steak. To prepare for a full day of chic shopping, stroll in between 9am and 11am for *huevos con chorizo*

or pancakes with seasonal fruit alongside honest-to-goodness, high-octane coffee.

Food 8, Service 6, Atmosphere 7

Chanterelle, 2 Harrison Street (Hudson), Tribeca

Tel: 212 966 6960   www.chanterellenyc.com
Open: noon–2.30pm, 5.30–11pm. Closed Sun–Wed lunch. $130
French

Few restaurants in New York manage to be this elegant while having so much fun with their cuisine, and owners Karen and David Waltuck (also the chef) see to it that every element of the Chanterelle experience is cosset-

ing, romantic, and enlivening, as well as relatively carefree (if you don't count paying the bill at the end of the night). It's all about getting close to your dinner partner and being inspired in the striking, spacious dining room, with its marvelous Queen Anne chairs and tasteful floral arrangements, not to mention menu covers created by celebrated artists. The Waltucks were fine-dining trailblazers in Tribeca back in 1979, and have held a special place in the heart of gastronomes ever since for their hands-on approach and obvi-ous love of great food. Each dish is crafted according to David's precise, pristine visions… marinated loin of lamb with marjoram and mini moussaka; wild striped bass with charcuterie sauce; duck two ways with port and dried sour cherries.

Food 9, Service 9, Atmosphere 9

Cipriani Downtown, 376 West Broadway (Broome), Soho

Tel: 212 343 0999   www.cipriani.com
Open: daily, noon–midnight $90
Italian

If it's a scene you want, a scene you will get at this unabashedly celeb-centric hotspot, where pretty young things drip with diamonds next to barons, matinee idols, titans of industry, and what appears to be an epidemic of trust-funders. Rest assured, however, the food, at times, is on par with the flash. The casual sister of Uptown's legendary Harry Cipriani, this Soho spot – with its unmarked yellow awning and heated sidewalk area – offers a uniquely unguarded glimpse into how members of the jet set size each other up. Despite the challenge of its entitled regulars, the wait staff does its best to make you feel like you belong, and the well-executed pastas (split the corn and cheese cannelloni with your dinner partner), generous prime beef sirloin, and special diet section (claiming to help you to "Gain Weight Safely" – how Soho) do a decent job at justifying the hefty bill.

Food 7, Service 7, Atmosphere 8

Cookshop, 156 Tenth Avenue (W 20th St), Chelsea
Tel: 212 924 4440 www.cookshopny.com
Open: daily, 11.30am–3pm, 5.30pm–midnight (10pm Sun) $60
Modern American

A noteworthy newcomer to West Chelsea – an area now well populated with art galleries, hotspots, run-off boutiques from the Meatpacking District, and arguably some of the most beautiful walking streets in the city – this sunny space takes its aesthetic cues from a country farmhouse and its culinary nods from its sister spot, Noho's Five Points. Greenmarket, chemical-free ingredients and certified humane meats are prepared by methods of rotisserie, stone hearth, and grilling; stand-outs include house-cured Hudson

Valley venison sausage, spice-crusted bigeye tuna with cranberry beans, Catskill duck breast with parsley root puree, or local baby chicken served with roasted carrots and maple butter-slathered cornbread. While very comforting, it's not to be written off as comfort food. With an outdoor terrace that serves as a sun trap in summer and a bar, staffed by an attentive barman, where customers can simply perch pre-dinner for a cocktail, Cookshop is a welcome addition to the rapidly gentrifying area around 10th Avenue.

Food 8, Service 8, Atmosphere 8

Degustation Wine & Tasting Bar, 239 East 5th Street (Bowery), East Village
Tel: 212 979 1012
Open: 6–11pm. Closed Sundays. $60
French-Spanish Tapas

This 18-seater sits side-by-side with owner Jack Lamb's famed new-sushi house Jewel Bako, which made him — handsome nerd and devoted East Villager that he is — an unlikely champion of haute raw fish concoctions. Meanwhile, Degustation is overseen by prodigious young chef Wesley Genovart and has been winning over the city's top palates for his bold, reverential juxtapositions. Genovart may be playing with your food, but it's hardly a childish affair… expect four or five of the tapas-sized plates to take you on wild flights through surf and turf. The five-course tasting menu at $50 is a treat you must allow yourself… when a chef is grabbing this much attention, it's best to let him choose and show you what's he's got. The prestige of this young meeting of gastronomic minds must have the old masters quaking a bit.

Food 9, Service 8, Atmosphere 8

Del Posto, 85 Tenth Avenue (W 15th St), Meatpacking District
Tel: 212 497 8090
Open: noon–3pm, 5pm–11.30pm Mon–Sat; noon–10pm Sun $100
Italian

Whenever Mario Batali and Joe Bastianich team up for a new venture, we take note. Over the past decade, the pair has given us plenty to digest — Babbo, Lupa, Esca, Otto, and Casa Mono. At grand West Chelsea stand-out Del Posto, Bastianich's mother, TV chef and Felidia proprietor Lidia Bastianich adds her celebrity heft to the mix, and the results are groundbreaking. The owners' mission:

to test and push the limits of regional Italian food preparations, giving diners an experience that rivals that of the top French restaurants. Whether that is even possible remains to be seen, yet New York's high-minded diners are glad to lend their appetites to the quest. (Reserve well in advance.) Expect clever antipasti (roasted autumn veggies dotted with truffled hazelnuts; shallot and vinegar-kissed scallop carpaccio), spot-on orechiette or gnocchi (try the family-style tastings), and ambitious main dishes – ender venison with walnuts and sour plums, Romanesca braised *orata*, and several dishes to share, such as the hulking veal chop and fresh *misto di mare*.

Food 9, Service 9, Atmosphere 9

Etats-Unis, 242 East 81st Street (3rd Ave), Upper East Side
Tel: 212 517 8826
Open: daily, 6–10pm $60
Modern American

Simple, elegant décor, a buzzing open kitchen, and one of the Upper East Side's more agreeable waitstaffs lend themselves nicely to the terrific, experiment-heavy menu that changes daily. No longer the fabulous secret that

locals kept in their back pockets, this tiny gem gets downright cacophonous by second seating with an occasionally prissy clientele. But you won't mind much, once you've dug into its seasonal offering – anything from an herb and chili stuffed *chilaquile* or house-cured salmon gravlax to fragrant organic stuffed chicken and Indian spiced lamb shank. For a cheaper, calmer evening, head across the street to the Bar@Etats-Unis, where you'll find a lounge vibe, impressive wine-by-the-glass program, and diverse menu of comforting favorites (including one of the city's top mac 'n' cheese dishes).

Food 8, Service 8, Atmosphere 8

Fiamma, 206 Spring Street (Sullivan), Soho
Tel: 212 653 0100 www.brguestrestaurants.com
Open: noon–2.30pm, 5.30pm (5pm Sun)–11pm (midnight Fri/Sat, 10pm Sun).
Closed Sat–Sun lunch. $75
Italian

The high-minded fare and sex-bomb atmosphere of this much-beloved osteria has kept it popular and packed since opening in 2003. One of the most well-received offerings from über-restaurateur Steve Hanson, Fiamma (Italian for "flame") is a feast for the eyes – three levels of comfy panache, with banquette seats, a mirrored wall (to catch wandering eyes directed toward your

supermodel date), warm light, well-chosen art, and its *pièce de résistance*, the glass elevator. Tender veal ravioli arrives fragrant with rosemary oil in a ragout of summer squash; organic salmon is stepped up with pancetta and sweet corn; the cheese tasting is a fine way to finish. If the crowd seems too daunting, don't fret: you can always check upstairs, and see about snagging a seat at the sleek, classic bar.

Food 8, Service 7, Atmosphere 9

Frankie's 457 Spuntino, 457 Court St (Carroll Gardens), Brooklyn

Tel: 718 403 0033   www.frankiesspuntino.com
Open: 11am–11pm (midnight Fri) Mon–Fri; 11am–4pm, 5.30–11pm Sat–Sun
Italian $44

Ignore the fact that this tiny, tasteful dining room first drew A-list celebrities to a stretch of Court Street in Carroll Gardens where they never would have ventured before 2005. The jovial guys – two fellows named Frank, as logic would dictate – who opened this class-act neighborhood joint have

managed to create truly unique Italian flavors in the middle of one of the most Italian neighborhoods in all the five boroughs (Al Capone was baptized around the corner). The menu is organic and market-driven. The handsome bar is well manned, and the wine list is prime. The meatballs, with their pine nuts and raisins, are to die for. Order any combo of the crostini bites and vegetable antipasti (Jerusalem artichokes are superbly prepared) and you'll be floored. Bread from the famous Sullivan Street bakery is lovingly manipulated. All in all, entirely worth venturing to Brooklyn for... and while you're here, stroll Smith Street for some chic home wares!

Food 8, Service 7, Atmosphere 8

Freeman's, Freeman Alley (Rivington) Lower East Side

Tel: 212 420 0012   www.freemansrestaurant.com
Open: daily, 11am–11.30pm $55
Northern European-influenced American

To the delight of refined hipsters citywide, this discreet haven, with all of its haute-hunting lodge charm, skims neither on atmosphere nor menu preparations, celebrating the simplicity of classic American and English gastronomy while drawing out the highest potential in its ingredients. Beneath the watchful eyes of hunting trophies (taxidermy is so in these days), the sexy crowd chatters at wooden tables while munching through eye-pleasing plates of triple-cheese macaroni, "Devils on Horseback" (blue-cheese stuffed prunes wrapped in bacon), the mixed grill (featuring rosemary lamb sausage, pork loin, and boar sausage), and seared filet mignon dabbed with horseradish cream and roasted onions. Particularly good is Freeman's at brunch time, where hungover locals feast on authentic beef brisket hash, and soul-satisfying skillet eggs arrive bubbling with bacon, spinach, and Gruyère cheese, accompanied by a skillfully prepared Bloody Mary.

Food 8, Service 7, Atmosphere 8

Gramercy Tavern, 42 East 20th Street (Broadway), Gramercy Park
Tel: 212 477 0777   www.gramercytavern.com
Open: noon–11pm (midnight Sat/Sun). Closed 4th July. $104
Modern American

Loved equally for its genteel atmosphere (soaring floral arrangements, murals by Robert Kushner, lovingly chosen antiques), the knowledge of its convivial staff, and the adventurous sensibilities of outstanding executive chef Michael Anthony and pastry chef Nancy Olson, Gramercy Tavern remains the most popular – and arguably the best – of Danny Meyer's impressive corral of restaurants. (Blue Smoke, Eleven Madison Park, Tabla, and Union Square Park are sister spots.) Anthony is a real talent, and satisfies with artistic plates such as open crab ravioli with razor clams and *escarole*, sweetbreads stepped up with sunchoke puree, the intimidating roasted rack of

pork and braised belly with leeks, and a lovely smoked lobster accompanied by celery root puree and a tangy pomegranate sauce. Get all of the circumstance, minus the pomp at the bar area – try it for a chic, more casual lunch – or simply stop in for a skillfully prepared cocktail such as the ginger and tonic at one of the most transporting bars in the city.

Food 10, Service 9, Atmosphere 9

Gin Lane, 355 W 14th Street (9th), Meatpacking District
Tel: 212 691 0555   www.ginlanenyc.com
Open: daily, 5pm–4am $64
American

Continuing New York's retro fascination with the prohibition era is Gin Lane, a speakeasy-style bar and restaurant in the center of the Meatpacking District. A quaint clapper-board front hides a darker more salubrious interior. The heavy mahogany bar at the front is tended by elegant mixologists serving up exquisite cocktails to a sophisticated crowd. Through a heavy velvet curtain lies the dining room, with a retractable roof allowing the room to breathe through New York's sultrier summer nights. The menu follows on the designed-retro theme with a more modern take on all-American classics ("Porterhouse steak," "pork chops", and "crab cakes"). A raw bar and

carefully selected wine list continue the sophisticated theme. Although the service can be a little over attentive, the food is excellent, the cocktails beautifully mixed and the interior wonderfully decadent. The bar stays open until 4am, so settle in and enjoy the neo-prohibition vibe before staggering home in the very early hours.

Food 8, Service 7, Atmosphere 8

The Harrison, 355 Greenwich Street (Harrison), Tribeca
Tel: 212 274 9310
Open: 5.30–10.30pm Mon–Sat; 5–9pm Sun $69
Modern American

One thing Jimmy Bradley and Danny Abrams do so well, be it at this Tribeca winner, Chelsea's memorable Red Cat, or the Mermaid Inn in the East Village, is offer comfortable luxury and unfettered fine fare without making a

big deal about it. Located just a little way up from the World Trade Center site, this handsome, understated (think: cherrywood, wainscoting) space plays home to some marvelous culinary feats from chef Brian Bistrong – peeky toe crab in mustard oil with avocado and grapefruit, skillet calf's liver in sherry reduction served alongside a bacon-onion torte, and almond crusted skate in apple cider sauce, to name a few. There is little to argue with at your meal's conclusion as fine coffee and a pistachio ice-cream-bedecked pear and caramel crisp lend itself to unhurried, satisfied conversation before you bid adieu to a night well executed.

Food 8, Service 7, Atmosphere 9

Lil' Frankie's, 19 First Avenue (E 1st St), East Village
Tel: 212 420 4900
Open: daily, 11am (10.30am (Sat/Sun)–2am (4am Fri/Sat, midnight Sun) $42
Italian – Pizza

While the East Village dining scene has gone remarkably upscale in recent years, it's nice to know that there are still spots that deliver on food yet remember the neighborhood's history. A glassed-off radio station (broad-

casting to East Village Radio; eastvillageradio.com) greets incoming diners, who gather (on weekend evenings in droves) to blow off steam with the scruffy boys and tough, sexy ladies who tend the tables, door, and bar. Within three rooms, each with a distinct character – one a brick taverna, the next a 1950s-style shoebox where the custom hearth resides, and the third a candlelit backroom adjoining a sliver of a garden patio – a casual, cool crowd delights at the stupendous Lil' Frankie's salad, the tender gnoc-chi and generous lasagna, the baked spinach with molten fontina, and thin-crusted pizzas artfully piled with fresh mozzarella chunks, and fine specialty toppings (the prosciutto-arugula, spicy salami, and the ortolana with zucchi-ni, eggplant, and mushrooms are all beyond). Pair it all with Peroni from the tap or any of the respectable Italian reds served in juice glasses, and your night is complete.

Food 7, Service 8, Atmosphere 8

Little Giant, 85 Orchard Street (Broome), Lower East Side
Tel: 212 226 5047   www.littlegiantnyc.com
Open: 11.30am (11am Sat/Sun)–3pm (4pm Sat/Sun), 6–11pm (midnight
Fri/Sat, 10pm Sun) $52
Modern American

Feeling at once like a roll-up-your-sleeves gathering place for fellow art-school alums and a smart, pomp-free eatery that holds your palate in high regard, this true-to-its-name, greenmarket-driven spot marries fresh, pre-

cisely cooked ingredients in exciting, unlikely ways. The "swine of the week" is always a tender offering (often involving "pork butt"... don't be fright-ened) amplified by seasonal fruits, herbs, and accompanied by a satisfying home-made biscuit of buttermilk and chives. The heirloom tomato, *burrata*, and basil salad is cool and palate-pleasing. *Cavatelli* with sage and pine-nut pesto are full and tender, kicked up with ricotta and port raisins. Pace your-self for desserts... The "Three maids a' milking" cheese plate, sinful bread pudding, and good old-fashioned Lower East Side egg cream seal the deal on a meal well done.

Food 8, Service 7, Atmosphere 8

Mary's Fish Camp, 64 Charles Street (W 4th), West Village
Tel: 646 486 2185   www.marysfishcamp.com
Open: noon–3pm, 6–11pm. Closed Sundays. $54
Seafood

There are two hands-down-marvelous American seafood houses in the West Village: Mary's, and the legendary Pearl Oyster Bar on Cornelia Street (where Fish Camp owner Mary Redding was once a partner). While both serve up supremely satisfying, classic fish dishes, something about the vibe at

Mary's – with its rounded bar; hip, friendly wait staff; and window-walled view onto chic, well-traversed West 4th Street – makes it as worthy a destination as any downtown. Once you're seated and reading the hand-scrawled specials board, you can't go wrong… reverentially seasoned chowder, salt-crusted shrimp, and Canadian steamers give way to Louisiana crabs au gratin, artfully constructed lobster rolls (perhaps the city's best), and pan-seared Arctic char fillet.

Food 8, Service 6, Atmosphere 7

Mercadito, 179 Avenue B (E 11th St), East Village

Tel: 212 529 6490

Open: noon–3pm, 5.30pm–midnight (1am Fri/Sat, 11pm Sun/Mon). Closed
Mon/Tues lunch $48

Mexican

For a breezy evening of tangy fresh fruit margaritas (giving the illusion of
health), world-class guacamole (several varieties in fact, available in tasting
form), superfresh ceviches – also available in a tasting – and a selection of
some of the most satisfying Mexican in the East Village (or beyond), stroll

past the hip crowds pouring out of the bars and bodegas of Avenue B and
settle at either of the transporting dining rooms for friendly service and
dishes that deliver. Sure, for a second it feels like you're sitting in Mexican
World at the Epcot Center, but hey. It's a hoot, and the cute waitstaff –
with smiles as wide as their accents are thick – make it as pleasurable an
experience as you're likely to have with a tiny taco stuffed in your mouth.
Treat yourself and go for the "Ostiones Horneados" – baked blue point
oysters dolled up with bacon, Manchego cheese, and chili Habanero *aioli*.

Food 8, Service 8, Atmosphere 8

Momofuku Ssam Bar, 207 Second Avenue (E 13th St), Lower East Side

Tel: 212 254 3500 www.momfuku.com

Open: daily, 11am–midnight $50

Korean/Eclectic

A must for any trend-savvy foodie with a taste for adventure, this polished downtown cafeteria offers first-rate experiments in Korean (primarily carnivorous) flavors from wily chef David Chang, whose Momofuku Noodle Bar packs in pleasure-seekers around the corner on First Avenue. Adding decadence to the pan-Asian flavors are indulgent soul food influences: a selection of various southern country hams; grilled pork ribs with chili glaze. The *ssam*

– Asian-style steamed buns filled with pork, fish, or steak and rice bibb lettuce – burst forward with flavor, while a nice cross-section of fish, everything from roasted skate with lemon and brown butter to Santa Barbara uni with whipped tapioca, offer an option to diners not yet ready to dive into Chang's experimentation with offal (think: spicy honeycomb tripes; grilled veal sweetbreads). Late night, things get really good, and you never know what member of the local glitterati will be soaking up the juices next to you

Food 9, Service 7, Atmosphere 7

Nice Matin, 201 West 79th Street (Amsterdam), Upper West Side

Tel: 212 873 6423
Open: daily, 7am–midnight (11pm Sun) $56
Mediterranean

While the décor feels a bit over the top at times – like a Riviera resort stop trying really, really hard – the vibe is splendid and the overall dining experience is a decidedly adult-friendly salve for the kid-saturated Upper West Side. It's a bright, friendly Mediterranean brasserie in a neighborhood

93

starving for one, with one of the city's best al fresco scenes that draws a

great mix of newspaper-sharing couples, unassuming professionals, and classy intellectuals who swear by the talent of chef Andy D'Amico, formerly of the charming Sign of the Dove. Try it for brunch, bustling though it may be, or head in on a weekday night for a nice selection of appetizers (leeks vinaigrette, roasted beets and *chèvre*); thin niçoise pizzas; golden snapper with lemon sabayon, artichokes, and peppers; or the five-napkin burger with sauteed onions, Comte cheese *aioli*, and fries. The cherry on top of it all: the sublime service; these people were chosen with care, for sure.

Food 8, Service 8, Atmosphere 7

Perry Street, 176 Perry Street (West), West Village
Tel: 212 352 1900 www.jean-georges.com
Open: daily, noon–3pm, 5.30pm–midnight $75
Modern American

Everyone has something to say about the dramatic Richard Meier buildings overlooking the Hudson River in the West Village – who's bought in them, what construction is going on, when people will actually move in… One thing that's indisputable is that internationally acclaimed chef Jean-Georges Vongerichten has bestowed upon the first of the buildings a sleek, fine restaurant – his eighth NYC venture – offering the increasingly monied far-West Village an appropriately posh gathering place and giving critics of his far-flung culinary endeavors a chance to see him meditate on flavors, and take diners on a journey. Serenely set in white, beige, and tan, the space cen-

ters around a sophisticated bar area, offers 60 generous seats at banquettes and tables, and is attended by his coolest, most relaxed staff.

Food 9, Service 9, Atmosphere 8

Prune, 54 East 1st Street (1st Ave), East Village
Tel: 212 677 6221
Open: 11.30am (10am Sat/Sun)–3pm, 6–11pm (midnight Fri/Sat, 10pm Sun)
Modern American $65

Something about this pint-sized New American charmer clicked right off the bat, and has consistently drawn a discerning, devoted crowd of fashionable foodies to the chic little strip between First and Second Avenues (also

boasting such restaurants as the sexy Elephant, Aussie snack shop the Tuck Shop, and the Tasting Room). Celebrated chef Gabrielle Hamilton brings together marvelous

service, hints of decadence, a prevailing spirit of simplicity, and a winking knowledge that what's being presented is clever, satisfying, and unexpected. The bar conjures up superb renditions of classic cocktails (multiple variations on the Bloody Mary, for instance), and the waitstaff is one of the friendliest and coolest in town. In fact, every element of your evening at Prune makes you feel like an insider; perhaps that's why it's always packed, particularly at brunch. Try it for lunch, a new addition this year that combines the eatery's best features – the light that comes pouring in and Hamilton's personal touch from behind the stove.

Food 9, Service 7, Atmosphere 7

Public, 210 Elizabeth Street (Prince), Nolita
Tel: 212 343 7011 www.public-nyc.com
Open: 11am–3.30pm (Sat/Sun only), 6pm–1am (2am Fri/Sat) $90
World/American, with Down Under Influence

For a really fantastic date – one that really feels like a date, meaning a transporting venue, the right amount of candlelight, enough of an audience so things don't seem stage, food that invigorates the senses with its textures

and wonderful tastes – you can't do much better than Public. Located in the heart of Nolita, Public is the picture of "industrial chic," with its deconstructionist décor from award-winning design company AvroKO. Chef Brad Farmerie puts on a real show every night, his fare as beautiful as it is well conceived – full grilled scallops with sweet chili sauce and crème fraîche, pan-seared New Zealand snapper, shiitake-crusted New Zealand venison loin with peppered spinach. Brunch purists swear by its Sunday morning, no-reservations feast with its fresh-baked scones, Turkish eggs with garlic yogurt and Kirmizi Biber butter, and corn and saffron pancakes. Ask about the tiny adjacent wine lounge called the Monday Room... It's a sexy little tucked-away secret.

Food 8, Service 8, Atmosphere 8

Schiller's Liquor Bar, 131 Rivington Street (Norfolk), Lower East Side

Tel: 212 260 4555   www.schillersny.com
Open: 11am (10am Sat/Sun)–1am (2am Thurs, 3am Fri/Sat) $55
Pan-Euro Comfort Food

While the expense account set has certainly clued itself in to this lively, white-tiled bistro from ever-clever restaurateur Keith McNally, true foodies and sexy downtowners still dot the cacophonous room, utterly addicted to the well-executed offerings such as mustard-crusted seared salmon, the oth-

erworldly steak frites (try it with the *Maître d'* butter), and authentic Welsh rarebit with grilled tomato. Hitting Schiller's in the early evening – back when we used to all eat – is key, for you'll be elbow-to-razorsharp-elbow with an entitled bottle blonde by 10pm. But no matter... the comforting fare, accompanied by three classifications of wine (cheap, decent, and good) will have you drowning out your neighbors in no time. At the end of the day, it comes down to this: Schiller's, as much and perhaps more than any of McNally's establishments, makes New York dining feel sexy and fun –

something it has been and always can be, as long as we all don't take it so seriously.

Food 8, Service 7, Atmosphere 7

Spigolo, 1561 Second Avenue (E 81st St), Upper East Side
Tel: 212 744 1100
Open: daily, 5.30–11pm (10pm Sun/Mon) $70
Italian

Helmed by handsome husband-and-wife team Scott and Heather Fratangelo, this maddeningly popular Upper East Side anomaly (rare in the neighborhood for its seductively simple exposed brick décor and a vibe that insists you leave your attitude out on the sidewalk of 81st Street) serves authentic trattoria flavors, reverentially prepared by chef Scott. (Hostess Heather doubles as the world-class pastry chef, who eschews tradition in favor of ever-

changing, soul-satisfying treats that borrow as much from American comforts as from by-the-book Italian confections.) Scott's melt-away sheep's milk ricotta gnocchi is now legendary, and his flavorful preparations of tender, brick-roasted baby chicken, Atlantic cod, and Tuscan-style grilled strip steak hit the mark without being heavy-handed. The six-course, wine-pairing tasting menu will cost you and your guests $95 each, but it's a true treat, one worth considering. It is not cheap, but hey, it's nice when an establishment knows its worth… and don't try to score a weekend night table without a reservation. You won't get in, and then you'll have to venture far out of the neighborhood for an experience that's even near comparable.

Food 9, Service 8, Atmosphere 7

The Spotted Pig, 314 West 11th Street (Greenwich), West Village

Tel: 212 620 0393 www.thespottedpig.com
Open: daily, noon (11am Sat/Sun)–2am $70
British & Italian

The enthusiasm with which New York has embraced this gastro-pub, nestled far into the sleepy West Village, has been astonishing. Perhaps it's the

Anglophile nature of your average Manhattan sophisticate; maybe it's just that the now-legendary sheep's ricotta gnudi with brown butter and sage renders diners powerless. Whatever the reason, its chef, April Bloomfield, and designer, Ken Friedman (both co-owners), have raised "bar food" to epic proportions, and the nightly lines follow suit. Insiders know that lunch is the way to savor the space properly, or perhaps late-late night (the kitchen closes at 2am nightly). There is, mercifully, a second dining floor that doubles occa-

sionally as a party space, so on average, at any time, a hundred or so diners are chuckling, sharing plates, and claiming they discovered the place before anyone else. Regardless, whether you're packed in or have it all to yourself, devouring a Rocquefort cheese-bedecked burger with a cold glass of stout beneath the pressed tin ceiling is haute, relaxed gastronomic sublimity.

Food 8, Service 7, Atmosphere 8

Suenos, 311 West 17th Street (8th Ave), Chelsea

Tel: 212 243 1333
Open: daily, 5–11pm (midnight Thurs–Sat) $46
Mexican

Tucked away on a sleepy Chelsea street, this bustling hideaway, once popu-
lated with couples from tryst-conducive Alley's End, thrives on energy and
spice, both from the clientele – who drink, sup, and flirt with abandon – and
the potent offerings of chef Sue Torres (formerly of Rocking Horse Café
around the corner), a stand-out in her field and a formidable manipulator of

Mexican flavors. Heat-seekers can opt for the chili tasting menu ($50 per
person), which will have you signaling for more water in five inspired ways,
but feel free to close your eyes and point at the menu. Try the grilled veggie
and Finger Lake goat cheese enchiladas, avocado leaf crusted tuna with
peanut mole, or lobster-and-corn fritters, you'll be a happy camper. The
crowd is perpetually sexy, and the fruity environs – fuchsia and peach walls
offset by flattering lighting, mirrors, and a skylight; enveloping banquettes, a
dramatic terrarium – inspire the histrionics to stretch deep into the night.
Potent bar specials will ensure that you stumble home (make sure you have
cab fare handy).

Food 8, Service 8, Atmosphere 9

Sweetwater, 105 North 6th Street, Williamsburg, Brooklyn
Tel: 718 963 0608
Open: noon (11.30am Sat)–midnight (2am Fri/Sat) $47
Modern American/Eclectic

A haven for genuine and faux Brooklyn foodies (some Manhattanites do like
to pose), Sweetwater is homey, reminiscent of old New York, and a simply
gorgeous arena in which outstanding eclectic American fare is served. When

the owners took over the space in 2004, they amped up its longstanding charms – floor tiles, bar, and pressed tin ceiling and walls – and brought in reverential flourishes such as inviting burgundy banquettes and photos from mid-century NYC. Once inside, diners settle in and get satiated by a medley of eclectic flavors: Georgia peaches marinated in lemon on a bed of arugula, goat cheese, and candied pecans; red chard and smoked bacon-stuffed organic chicken, "bronzed" on goat cheese mash; and chili-rubbed pork tenderloin with Kentucky bourbon sauce, caramelized apple, and fried shallots. The food is no joke, while the service is no frills and fabulous.

Food 8, Service 8, Atmosphere 8

Telepan, 72 West 69th St (Columbus), Upper West Side
Tel: 212 580 4300   www.telepan-ny.com
Open: 11.30am (11am Sat/Sun)–2.30pm, 5–11pm (11.30pm Fri/Sat) $75
American

Polished American country fare is artfully prepared and reverentially presented at this much-beloved Upper West Side offering from chef-owner Bill Telepan, an alum of Judson Grill, Le Cirque, Gotham Bar & Grill, and the three-Michelin-star French marvel Alain Chapel in France. Telepan turns to the freshest greenmarket ingredients and creates a vast, frequently shifting menu of soul-satisfying Americana flavors, from foie gras donuts and poached egg and frisée salad with scrapple to the surprising short rib and beet green pierogi and entrees such as buttermilk-braised bass with dill potatoes and pork "four-ways," with mashed peas and grits. While the wait, even with a reservation, can be trying, the experience – the space, a soft-lit,

gently decorated townhouse; the service, accommodating yet out of your hair – is worth your patience.

Food 9, Service 8, Atmosphere 8

WD-50, 50 Clinton Street (Stanton), Lower East Side
Tel: 212 477 2900
Open: daily, 6–11.30pm (10pm Sun) $67
Modern American

Wylie Dufresne has revamped the American culinary landscape, introducing new techniques and combining unlikely flavors in ways that are as endlessly entertaining to discuss as they are delightful to sample. This handsome, unstuffy eatery on Clinton Street, up the block from where chef Dufresne first garnered attention as the chef at 71 Clinton Fresh Food, sets a subtle

stage for this maestro's passionate displays, with its exposed beams, terra-cotta walls, aquatic murals, and understated, comfy banquettes. The staff is well educated in the tastes and techniques exiting the kitchen. With artistry and aplomb, Dufrense offers ravishing bites of corned duck on a rye crisp, heightened with purple mustard horseradish cream; combines scallops, king oyster mushrooms, and dried apricots; uses cheddar and apple to up the ante on tender braised short ribs with brussel sprouts; and so on. The nine-course tasting menu for $115 is a true treat for a bona fide foodie.

Food 10, Service 9, Atmosphere 8

drink...

There are a million and one ways to have fun in New York, but this is the *Hedonist's Guide*, after all, and oftentimes that means imbibing like you really mean it. So we thought, *What makes for a truly satisfying night of drinking?* The specifics are as diverse as the people who come here, but there are a few general rules we like to follow. Intoxication, and the subsequent loss of inhibition (or bodily function, depending on who you are), calls for an environment in which you are comfortable and where you are surrounded by stimulating folks with whom you can cut loose without fear of reproach. If you love to howl at your friends' jokes, for example, don't go to the Burp Castle on East 7th Street, where it's all about the worshipful consumption of beer, and the decibel level is kept to a low hum by the staff. If you love the velvet rope scene and 'getting in' really gets you off, don't be talked into Welcome to the Johnsons on Rivington Street… You won't be happy and your vibe will be a real downer to the hipsters that flock there.

That said, there is a perfect place for you out there. The more honest you are about what and who you are, the better time you will have, so think on it…Do you like your crowds diverse, laid-back, and young? Raucous and rowdy? Sophisticated and knowledgeable in the ways of spirits? Absolutely filthy rich? Each of these crowds get touched upon here, though we do have a real penchant for temples of mixology like Little Branch, Employees Only, and Pegu Club. They aren't so snotty that you can't relax, though their drinks are primo and the atmosphere at any of them will instantly whisk you away to a different world – a world where fermented spirits are the firmament of society. Worry not if you're a pub-crawler or a high-rolling exec out to drink on the company's dime: You'll find something in here, too.

Being champion boozers, let us just say that it was painful to exclude many of our top-of-mind watering holes when crafting this guide. What we give you is a saucy slice of spirited fun… Chances are you'll have a grand time at any and all of these mentioned. If you don't, perhaps you'll consider these: The cool, clubby Campbell Apartment in Grand Central Terminal begs you to enjoy a nice brandy. Tao on East 58th Street, Blue Water Grill on Union Square West, or Monkey Bar on East 54th Street provide a sexy after-work crowd. Both the Old Town Tavern and Pete's Tavern in the Flatiron District offer noteworthy bar fare and throwback environs, while Lower East Side and Alphabet City music venues the Living Room, Mo Pitkin's, the Delancey and Mercury Lounge draw terrific acts of many stripes. There are scene-y martini-swilling stopovers like Rande Gerber's Underbar at the W Union Square hotel, the excellent Lucy at ABC Carpet & Home, Level V at Vento restaurant in the Meatpacking District, and velvet rope legend Bungalow 8 – where trashy behavior among the celebrity set is par for the course and getting in without knowing someone is unlikely. Downtown hipsters love Sweet and Vicious or Good World, while Tribeca mon-

eymakers still manage to make the Odeon a place to be seen. Not to forget the Uptowners, you get get your kicks and sips on the Upper East Side at Baraonda, Iggy's Bar, Luke's Bar & Grill, or Vudu Lounge, while Irish pub fun awaits on the Upper West at Emerald Inn or George Keeley.

If *nothing* here floats your boat, wear some comfy shoes and do some investigation on your own.

Arlene's Grocery, 95 Stanton St (Ludlow), Lower East Side
Tel: 212 995 1652 www.arlenesgrocery.net
Open: daily, 6pm–4am

This adrenaline-fueled music venue on the Lower East Side is a great place to let your hair down... but don't show up with your collar turned up. It's a place to give into the sound of emo, punk, and indie bands – and maybe let it take you completely over on Monday night during their rock and roll

karaoke, complete with a live band. A former grocery store and butcher shop, Arlene's has a reputation for booking top homespun bands – not to mention for welcoming big-name acts back in, who are humble enough to perform for the $7 cover charge (Michael Stipe and Dashboard Confessional). The Butcher Bar out front is a good place to kick back with a beer, hear new tracks, and scope the room for new fashion trends.

Art Bar, 52 Eighth Avenue (W 4th St), Chelsea
Tel: 212 727 0244
Open: daily, 4pm–4am

If you're down in Chelsea and looking for a pretense-free gin and tonic, draft beer, or Martini – served at human prices – the Art Bar is a refreshing hang-out, drawing in a pleasant mix of tipplers who use honey more often than vinegar to get by you on their way to the bar. The front room, with its circular banquettes and classic everyman bar picks up in volume by mid-evening. So perhaps opt for the back room, with its low lighting, working fireplace, and flickering candles – plus a Pop Art "Last Supper" hanging on

the wall – where you'll be able to whisper sweet nothings and get dazed well into the night without a lot of traffic spoiling the mood.

Aspen, 30 West 22nd Street (5th Ave), Chelsea

Tel: 212 645 5040 www.aspen-nyc.com

Open: 6pm–midnight. Closed Sundays.

The city has been gripped with hunting-lodge/ski-chalet fever for the past year of two, with more mounted stag and elk heads than you can shake a stick at. But nowhere does it feel more appropriate than at this sleek hotspot, where barn wood and Aspen birch details, Lucite taxidermy trophies, Colorado charms, and rustic flourishes give it a woodsy feel, amplified

by the kiss of amber candlelight. Doubling as a popular restaurant among the jet-set crowd, Aspen is a bit of a model-PR maven haven, and suffers all the trappings of that. But catch it on the right night and it's nothing but sexy and sleek. There is a nice selection of specialty cocktails, though you may need to cash in your Rolex to pay the bill at the end of the night.

Bar Veloce, 175 Second Avenue (E 11th St), East Village
Tel: 212 260 3200 www.barveloce.com
Open: daily, 5pm–3am

Long gone are the days when East Village bar life hinged on binge-drinking, punk music, and barely-21-style debauchery. This soothing, narrow wine bar, for example, has played host to a cross-section of smartly dressed drinkers

since 2000, offering excellent *panini*, *bruschetta*, meats, and cheeses alongside a stellar, affordable by-the-glass Italian wine menu (*sake*, *grappa*, and such are now available). The blond wood bar is a great place to pull up a chair and catch up with a friend or two (no more) who can appreciate the throwback black-and-white films being projected on the back wall. If you're straight and in Chelsea looking for a proper drink, head to the larger sister spot on 21st Street and Seventh Avenue.

Barracuda, 275 West 22nd Street (8th Ave), Chelsea
Tel: 212 645 8613
Open: daily, 4pm–4am

For a gay bar experience that manages not to be too campy, too déclassé, or too snobby – yet sits smack dab in the middle of Chelsea – head to this low-lit, decade-old watering hole where square-jawed barkeeps (who keep their shirts on, believe it or not) serve moderately priced drinks to good-natured regulars who yuk it up, do a fair amount of flirting, and lap the two rooms – the rear is a maze of worn-in couches, kitsch end tables, and lamps where dizzy waiters try not to spill trays of Martinis while rounding the

pool table and squeezing past over-muscled patrons. The décor changes with the season, so there's usually a fun reason to check back in.

Bemelmans Bar, Carlyle Hotel, 35 East 76th Street (Madison), Upper East Side

Tel: 212 744 1600 www.thecarlyle.com
Open: daily, noon–11.30pm

Loosen your tie and settle back with a brandy as choice pianists and cabaret performers set the night to music. You'll want to look a little polished, just to fit in with the fat billfold crowd, but the class-act servers will put a smile on your face no matter how you arrive. Famous for its Central Park animal mural by famed writer and illustrator Ludwig Bemelmans (author of *Madeleine*), this spot is a romantic slice of clubby, old New York – and the cocktail list, crafted by master mixologist Brian Van Flanders, will please even

the most snobbish of cocktail purists. Try the Gin-gin Mule – gin with ginger beer, fresh mint, and lime juice – or a champagne-topped mojito with bitters, the Old Cuban.

Black & White, 86 East 10th Street (3rd Ave), East Village
Tel: 212 253 0246
Open: daily, 6pm–4am

For a good flirt, a strong drink, and an eclectic mix of creative professionals in their mid-20s and 30s, this amber-lit canteen fits the bill nicely. Enter down a few steps off a quiet East Village block (beneath a striped awning where the smokers huddle), and try to score a stool at the far end of the

bar to survey the crowd, or pour into a plush banquette with your buddies. It is not the most spacious spot in town, but that adds to the appeal, as you're bound to rub up against someone eye-catching. The bartenders know what they're doing, so order with confidence.

Black Door, 127 West 26th Street (6th Ave), Chelsea
Tel: 212 645 0215
Open: daily, 4pm–4am

On any given night, you'll find gabby yet well-behaved groups of PR gal pals, financiers, journalists, grad students, and fashion execs letting their hair down and enjoying the civilized tone set by the chummy bartenders and servers at the Upper Chelsea anomaly. Hang your coat on one of the many

wall hooks and hop into one of the plentiful seats – particularly nice are the two-seater tables across the bar, offering a prime view of the flirtatious crowd. The votives cast a kind glow on everyone involved, and neighborhood dogs lower the room's blood pressure.

Blind Tiger, 281 Bleecker Street (Jones), West Village
Tel: 212 462 4682   www.blindtigeralehouse.com
Open: daily, 4pm–4am

When the original Blind Tiger, on 10th Street and Hudson, was cruelly replaced by a Starbucks, the owners decided to expand their reach and sensibilities. They researched fine coffee roasting techniques, enlisted one of their bartenders – conveniently a French Culinary Institute graduate – to craft an artisanal, alcohol-friendly menu, and bought up 150-year-old farmhouse wood to trick out their new space with well-worn charm. The results

were better than they could have imagined... new and improved, this Blind Tiger is one of the most comforting, well-executed pubs in the city; a café by day and microbrew paradise by night that neighborhood characters of every stripe have embraced. The 30 drafts include many a strange brew, indeed.

bOb, 235 Eldridge Street (Stanton), Lower East Side
Tel: 212 529 1807
Open: 7.30pm–4am. Closed Mondays.

Fun and frisky, this brick-walled cube is a great place to steal away for a sweaty dance session, although the crowds get intense at times. The roster of DJs is really ace, unleashing a nightly litany of hip-hop, reggae, and R&B.

Most nights get packed by one o'clock, so be prepared so suck in that gut and move fish-like through the undulating room on the way to the bathroom. Early evenings are an entirely different brand of fun, when you can admire some of the local artwork adorning the walls and chat up the sex kitten bartenders as they ply you with decently strong drinks.

Bowlmor Lanes, 110 University Place (E 13th St), Village
Tel: 212 255 8188
Open: daily, 11am–1am (3am Mon, 2am Thurs, 4am Fri/Sat)

The kitsch factor is high and the lanes aren't the cheapest at this University Place bastion of 10-pin glory, which dates back to 1938 and boasts a big-

money revamp in the late 1990s. But remember this: bowling, whether you're good, bad, or worse, is very amusing, and tends to get more so the more heavily you drink. So, if you and your group tire of velvet ropiness, rent a lane or two – or simply kick back at the Lanes's throwback lounge and order round after round of shots. There are often corporate events or magazine theme parties to contend with, but that's OK – you're all there for the same reason: to wear rented shoes and triumph over drunken comrades.

Brandy Library, 25 North Moore Street (Varick), Tribeca
Tel: 212 226 5545
Open: daily, 4am–4pm

An amber-lit playground for whiskey's most astute enthusiasts, this handsome temple of tippling features a vast array of spirits – aged 10, 12, 20 years or more – in a posh downtown setting with fine service, plush leather

seating, and a clubby, chummy atmosphere that harkens back to mid-century and is sorely missing in today's drinking landscape. It's study hall, all grown up, as brandies line the shelves – complete with a ladder to reach the offerings up top – and folks who know a good gulp when they taste it refine their knowledge with Saturday evening tastings and Tuesday night spirit school. Tartare, caviar, "lambs in a blanket," and superior charcuterie and cheese plates are on hand, in case your drunken stomach gets to growling.

Club Macanudo, 26 East 63rd Street (Madison), Upper East Side
Tel: 212 752 8200 www.clubmacanudonyc.com
Open: 5pm–1am (1.30am Weds–Sat). Closed Sundays for private events.

Well ventilated and maintained, this tobacco enthusiast's haven is one of the few city establishments where you can still light up inside – and is also a popular dining and mingling spot for a fresh-faced cross-section of smokers and non-smokers. Offering an impressive, reasonably priced selection of

cigars as well as a well-stocked top shelf bar, the Club is a well-preserved slice of social history – and its ritzy address ensures that those elbows you're rubbing are upper crust, all the way. The specialty drink menu includes decadent Martinis, such as the knock-out Havana Martini with (Bacardi Orange, Limon, and Coco, as well as pink lemonade), and the opulent Sixty-Third Street Martini – a dreamy cognac and pear concoction – that will run you $63.

Cub Room, 131 Sullivan Street (Prince), Soho

Tel: 212 677 4100 www.cubroom.com
Open: daily, 11am–4am

This homey, brick-lined lounge, located on one of the less hectic corners of
Prince Street in Soho, offers an admirable selection of global wines, tequilas,
vodka, and Scotch (there's a good shot they have your brand) plus a con-

vivial atmosphere, where you'll be comfortable enough to let your hair
down and flirt with local off-duty shopkeepers yet still feel like an adult. A
light menu is available in the lounge that includes satisfying spring rolls,
bruschetta, thin-crusted pizzettas, and calamari, plus a special late-night
menu for quelling a hard-partying hunger. Wash it back with a Greta Garbo
cocktail (cognac, Cointreau, champagne, and a little lemon) or a Chinatown
(pear-infusion vodka Martini with lychee puree and lychee liqueur.)

d.b.a., 41 First Avenue (E 3rd St), East Village

Tel: 212 475 5097 www.drinkgoodstuff.com
Open: daily, 1pm–4am

With over 150 beers – draft selections changing daily – and a vast selection
of vodkas, Scotches, bourbons, and tequilas, this cheery East Village drinking
hall makes an art out of making you feel at home and getting you inebriated.
The crowd gets a smidge rowdy by midnight (who can blame them?), so
you'll fit right in as you do a little taste-testing at their wood booths or
smooshed up against the bar. On Mondays, come in and enjoy a complimentary artisanal cheese tasting, then make it a point to ditch your brunch

dates early on Sundays and check out their celebration of the Bloody Mary, complete with complimentary papers, bagels, and lox.

Ear Inn, 326 Spring Street (Greenwich), West Village
Tel: 212 226 9060 www.jamesbrownhouse.com
Open: daily, noon–4am

Neighborhood locals cherish this quirky landmark bar, established in 1817, which is said to be the oldest in Manhattan. (Rumor has it that a sign once read "Bar, Inn," but part of the "b" got cut off and resulted in its present moniker.) With its low ceilings and knick-knack clutter, it's a wonderful place to get cozy for an evening – although weekend crowds can be hop-up-and-down infuriating. Its warped floors and seemingly slanted bartop make you feel drunk even before you've reached your third pint, so if you're feeling woozy, order from their no-frills bar menu. (A few fries can go a long way.)

There's a craggy gentility about the place that you just have to love, and chances are one visit will inspire another. Catch live music on weekday evenings, and dig the Saturday afternoon poetry readings, a decades-long tradition.

Eight Mile Creek, 240 Mulberry Street (Prince), Nolita
Tel: 212 431 4635   www.eightmilecreek.com
Open: daily, 4pm (11am Sat/Sun)—4am

These Aussies have charmed the well-fitting pants off of this fashionable neighborhood, with its boisterous, flirtatious staff; tasty bar bites such as "kanga skewers" (kangaroo with mountain berry ketchup), baby meat pies, prawn dumplings — even Vegamite sandwiches; and an impressive selection of booze. Aside from the numerous beers on tap, they offer a very nice assortment of Aussie and New Zealand wines, as well as a kicky cocktail menu

with everything from the Mulberry Captain (Captain Morgan's spiced rum, champagne, lime, and mint), to the Kiwi vodka Martini (with Midori, pineapple and lemon juices), to cheap sangria that will leave you cross-eyed. In summer months, the back garden is a sweet spot to drink the day away. (Summer Sundays host a barbecue chef cook-off.)

Employees Only, 510 Hudson Street (W 10th), West Village
Tel: 212 242 3021   www.employeesonlynyc.com
Open: daily, 6pm—4am

Precise mixology is the name of the game at this swank West Side throwback saloon, where you're greeted by a fortune teller in a bona fide mystic's alcove, while moustache-sporting barkeeps – each with years of training, most from legendary cocktail house Pravda – concoct drinks ranging from

sweet to vicious, flirtatious to mind-numbing. Let's start with the Ginger Smash, the house specialty, where muddled cranberries and ginger root get a sinful shake through Beefeater Wet gin and apple liqueur. It will make you consider dropping vodka forever. Then, there's the Billionaire's Cocktail, a smooth blend of Bakers bourbon, lemon juice, home-made grenadine, and absinthe bitters. These boys are big on the complexities of gin, and can use it in the most exciting of ways, so keep that factoid in mind when ordering. Other virtues: dreamy Deco décor, a seasonal outdoor patio, and a decent late-night menu that goes 'til 4am.

Flatiron Lounge, 37 West 19th Street (5th Ave), Flatiron
Tel: 212 727 7741
Open: daily, 5pm–2am (4am Thurs–Sat)

It's a little foreboding from the outside, with its scene-obscuring curtain covering the window, but once inside experience a sparkly, sexy affair; a true adult's lounge where classic New York cocktails get reverential treatment and conversation flows freely among jet-setters, power brokers, and glitzy locals. Mixologist Julie Reiner put her heart into crafting a dreamy cocktail menu with selections ranging from a flight of three Martinis to notable drinks from top city establishments. The hibiscus swizzle is an African berry-infused gin winner drizzled with hibiscus syrup, while the Floridita Daiquiri presents its white rum, maraschino liqueur, and juices of grapefruit and lime with cheeky aplomb. You could imagine swank stars of yesteryear sidling up

the long mahogany bar, which was built in 1927 and originally situated at the Ballroom, a regular Sinatra hang-out. Jazzy and very swish, indeed.

Heathers, 506 East 13th Street (Avenue A), East Village
Tel: 212 254 0979
Open: 6pm–2am Sun–Wed, 4pm–4am Thurs–Sat

Plagued by noise complaints from upstairs neighbors, this well-meaning *boîte* in the far East Village – run by a sweet-faced moppet named, you guessed it, Heather – probably won't be blowing out its speakers when you stroll in, but the scene will inevitably be groovy. Low energy hipsters and the guys who like to hit on them can't get enough of the *laissez-faire* ambience and

classic rock soundtrack, not to mention the cheap pricetag on the well-mixed drinks. It's not trying to be anything more than a great gathering place for Heather, her friends, and the people who seemingly should be her friends, and we just like that. So if you feel like you and Heather might get along – a.k.a. you love your jeans, you know all the words to at least one Led Zeppelin album, and you'd rather talk literature than *Star* magazine – then this is your place.

Joe's Pub, The Public Theater, 425 Lafayette Street (E 4th St), Noho
Tel: 212 539 8777
Open: daily, 6pm–2am

A justifiably popular institution attached to the venerable Public Theater, Joe's Pub – named for theater legend Joseph Papp – is a cool cat lounge, meticulously run, that showcases an extensive cross-section of jazz, cabaret, and comedy performance. While sitting rapt as any number of virtuosi vie for adoration, audience members delight at the comfy velvet seating and subtle, sleek flourishes, and pore over a clever cocktail list and bar menu. A

Huckleberry Martini marries huckleberry-infused vodka with lime, pome-granate juice, and ginger ale, while port wine and champagne commingle to create the Lady Macbeth. There is a $12 food minimum per person if snack-ing, and eats range from rustic *panini* to ample meatballs, burgers, pastas, and fish.

Lenox Lounge, 288 Lenox Avenue (E 126th St), Harlem
Tel: 212 427 0253 www.lenoxlounge.com
Open: daily, noon–4am

A Harlem jazz mainstay since 1939, this storied club was a favorite venue
for Billie Holiday, John Coltrane, and Miles Davis. (Malcolm X and Langston
Hughes were regulars in the crowd.) Mercifully, its 2000 redo didn't steal its
classic charms; rather, it dusted off a true nightlife jewel that still manages to

impress in terms of stage talent, ambience, and soul food menu. Order up
some Poor Man's Gumbo or stuffed Cajun shrimp with black eyed peas,
macaroni and cheese, or collard greens and settle in as regular weekly acts
set your feet to tapping (Monday nights feature the superb Patience Higgins)
and special performances delight the appreciative, reverential crowds.

Little Branch, 20 Seventh Avenue (Leroy), West Village
Tel: 212 929 4360
Open: daily, 7pm–3am

A sparkling jazz joint from Sunday to Wednesday, the subterranean hideaway
(watch your step while descending) features some of the most inventive
cocktails in town. Owned by the same obsessive mixologist who brought
Milk & Honey to the cocktail-obsessed throngs of upper echelon
Manhattan, Little Branch features a similar cocktail menu – polished renditions of high-octane classics with the freshest of juices, made more special
by hand-cut ice. The punches are potent, mojitos marvelous, caiprinhas killer,
and daiquiris surprisingly subtle. Little Branch's bar staff is trained to the hilt

and smartly dressed – but be sure not to snap their suspenders while they shake your Manhattan.

N, 33 Crosby Street (Broome), Nolita
Tel: 212 219 8856
Open: 11.30am (noon Sun)–8.30pm (9pm Fri/Sat, 6pm Sun). Closed Monday.

This place gets packed to the hilt, so get here early and score a seat with a good conversationalist – because you are going to be here a while once the tiny tapas bites start pouring from the kitchen and your magnificent pitcher of sangria, amplified by perfect fruit cubes, starts warming you up. Their Spanish charcuterie plate, flavorful calamari, and marinated mushrooms are

particularly good. Beautiful servers with even more beautiful accents keep you smiling for as long as you can hold on to your seat (the best are at the back bar… right by the kitchen). The communal bathroom is a kick, too, with its cool blue tiles and pedestal sink.

The Otheroom, 143 Perry St (Washington), West Village
Tel: 212 645 9758   www.theroomsbeerandwine.com
Open: daily, 5pm–2am (4am Wed–Sat)

Though it only carries wines and beer – and won't accept your credit card – you won't miss the spirits when you sink into the genial vibe that exists nightly at this largely tourist-free spot. The convivial attitude starts with the waitstaff – a cute bunch that spares us any pretense – and continues with its

T-shirt and jeans-clad clientele. Be careful not to sink too deeply into one of the couches, otherwise you might not move for an hour or so. The knowingly selected international wines will please most vinophiles, and the bottled beer selection is vast. Best of all, the dim lighting off the brick walls makes you look ten years younger – and considering the cuties who tend to wander through, that's a very good thing. If you're a smoker, the sidewalk bench out front makes for prime people-watching.

Pegu Club, 7 West Houston Street (Broadway), Soho
Tel: 212 473 7348   www.peguclub.com
Open: daily, 5pm–2am (4am Thurs–Sat)

The city's big cocktail snobs gave a collective sigh of relief when this handsome, second-floor lounge – named for a storied British colonial officer's club in late 19th-century Rangoon – opened its doors and offered a marvelously conceived drink menu; a transporting, Indochine-chic aesthetic; and a mission to mix every cocktail perfectly and maintain its integrity as you drink it (perfect ice cubes, glasses of proper size, proper storage and treat-

ment of mixers and garnishes). Impressive in its sincerity and flawless in its presentation, Pegu Club is the brainchild of Audrey Saunders, a student of mixologist Dale DeGroff who honed her knowledge and skills while running Bemelmans Bar at the Carlyle (see page 38). Now that she's got a chic playground all her own, she's hitting it out of the park.

The Rose Bar, Gramercy Park Hotel, 2 Lexington Avenue (E 21st St), Gramercy Park
Tel: 212 920 3300 www.gramercyparkhotel.com
Open: 5pm–4am. Closed Sundays and Mondays.

No plan is failsafe in the world of Manhattan nightlife. But when odds are stacked so far in your favor, as in the case of this stylish, Spanish-style salon on the ground floor of Ian Schrager's Gramercy Park Hotel (see Sleep),

things can go very, very right. Giants of the entertainment and media world flock to this airy, refined *boîte* conceived by artist Julian Schnabel, who custom-designed the furniture and selected important works by Cy Twombley, Warhol, Basquiat, and, yes, himself to grace the walls. An impressive hearth and billiards table give it a warm, clubby edge, and the adjoining Jade Bar is a continuation of the cool, only presented in a glowing green. Drinks aren't cheap but, goodness, are they made with flair.

Sortie, 329 West 51st Street (8th Ave), Hell's Kitchen

Tel: 212 265 0650 www.sortieny.com
Open: 5pm–2am (4am Fri/Sat). Closed Sun and Mon for private parties.

An awfully slinky spot for Hell's Kitchen, this deep red underground lounge gets to the point for traditional party-seekers looking for mind-numbing electro beats, pricey yet strong specialty cocktails, and a sleek décor that invites you to kick back and flirt. Complete with a private space at the rear, Sortie is a great meeting spot for Midtown, and its small plates menu –

bruschetta, spring rolls, *dim sum*, and such – is nicely presented. In fact, happy hour (5 to 7pm, and then again at midnight until 2am) features specially priced beers, Martinis, and wine, as well as a reduced price on some of their food.

Stone Rose, 4th Floor, Time Warner Center, 10 Columbus Circle (8th Ave), Upper West Side

Tel: 212 823 9769
Open: daily, 4pm–2am (midnight Sun)

A decidedly subdued lounge from nightlife superstar Rande Gerber (hubby to Cindy Crawford, the lucky dog), this posh playground inside the Time Warner Center boasts 5,500 square feet of schmoozing space, noteworthy neighbors such as Terrence Brennan and Michael Lomonaco, and dramatic, wall-length windows that look onto Central Park and the great city beyond it. Gerber sets a sexy stage, with rosewood paneling, plenty of candlelight,

marble floors, and a long, striking bar at which many a beauty dangles her stems. If you're peckish, the bar bites are mighty tasty – as are the barkeeps and servers. (Seems they have this habit of hiring only very, very sexy people. Strange!) If you've got reservations at any of the Center's remarkable eateries – Asiate, Masa, Per Se, Landmarc, Café Gray, Porter House New York, so on, so forth – this is the place to start… or finish, if you've get post-prandial energy for just one more.

Temple Bar, 332 Lafayette Street (Hudson), Noho
Tel: 212 925 4242
Open: 5pm–1am (2am Fri/Sat). Closed Sundays.

Sexy grown-ups engage in actual conversation – sometimes between friends or colleagues, sometimes gazing into a stranger's eyes – over classic and specialty cocktails, $8 pints of Grolsch, and bar bites ranging from spicy chicken wings to foie gras mousse. The merciful lighting and class act servers lend to the stolen-away vibe – its devotees don't want you knowing about it – while its impressive selection of gins and vodkas ensure you'll find a tipple to suit your taste. What makes it so unique is that it's lively without being a mob scene; it's private without being sordid. Beware if you are of the rowdy

sort: sometimes its polish can come off as pretension, so if you're looking to make a scene, go elsewhere.

Therapy, 348 West 52nd Street (8th Ave), Hell's Kitchen
Tel: 212 397 1700
Open: daily, 5pm–2am (4am Thurs–Sat)

Now that the gay community has left much of its former ghetto, Chelsea, to the straight gallery owner set and dug in its heels in Hell's Kitchen, a little polish is becoming more commonplace. It is, at least, at this popular Midtown hangout – formerly a carriage house, a warehouse, and a brothel

(not all at once) – where two floors of coolly lit lounge play host to mainstream gay professionals and younger Abercrombie types. Boy-toy bartenders grin and bear hordes of adoring customers ordering up – among the typical Martinis, light beers, and shots – specialty drinks such as the

127

Pavlov's Dog (Stoli Vanil, Midori, lemon sour, and pineapple juice), and Coitus Interruptus (Tanqueray 10, raspberry liqueur, grenadine, lemon, and champagne).

Zinc Bar, 90 West Houston Street (W Broadway), Soho
Tel: 212 477 8337 www.zincbar.com
Open: daily, 6pm–3.30am (2.30am Tue–Thurs & Sun)

Welcoming a zesty, ever-changing roster of performers to its stamp-sized stage, this jazz joint is big on celebrating emerging talent, and mixes up the genres on a nightly basis. Be prepared to share your personal space on weekend nights, as samba and bossa nova acts pack in an eclectic, enthusiastic clientele – although know you can always steal away to the back room to kick back and catch your breath. Talented bartenders blend tropical cock-

tails with precision, and the sexy red velvet vibe makes you feel like you're getting more than your $5-worth. (Yes, there's a $5 cover, plus a one-drink minimum for everyone, and a two-drink minimum for those seated for a show.) Well worth it, we'd say.

Zum Schneider, 107 Avenue C (E7th), East Village
Tel: 212 598 1098 www.zumschneider.com
Open: 5pm (1pm Sat/Sun)–1am (4am Fri/Sat)

As authentically Bavarian an experience as you are going to find anywhere in the five boroughs, this much-loved indoor-outdoor beer garden, owned and

operated by the multi-generational Schneider family, pours a superb selection of lagers, Pilsners, wheat beers, and dark brews to an appreciative, pleasure-seeking crowd of low-frills locals, off-the-boat Germans, and – as logic would dictate – urbanized frat boys. Freshly baked Bavarian pretzels, baked Camembert with lingonberry jam, and, yes, weiner schnitzel, are satisfying and authentic. There is sidewalk seating during sunnier months, while wood communal tables keep things chummy indoors.

snack...

It's non-stop action here in New York, and you need to keep your energy up. That means nibbling and noshing throughout the day – a true pleasure when the offerings are this fabulous and diverse. We barely scraped the surface of spots to stop in for a quick refuel.…There are many more where these came from.

The locals rely heavily on the 24-hour delis or *bodegas* that populate countless corners throughout the city. There, you'll find your chewing gum, bananas, ATMs, cigarettes, candy bars, light groceries, beverages, beer, newspapers, and Oreos. We heart 24-hour delis for their all-inclusiveness. But when you're only here for a short while, you need to snack in style. We have some of the best pizza in the world, so take advantage of the many pizza parlors selling pies and slices. There are the iconic street vendors selling hot dogs and pretzels… though, eeew. Opt for the haute hot dog creations of F&B on West 23rd Street or Crif Dogs on St. Mark's Place, instead. For dessert-o-philes, there's Rice to Riches on Spring Street, where rice pudding takes center stage; haute dessert spots like Chicalicious, Sundaes and Cones, and Room 4 Dessert; or ice cream joints like Emack & Bolio's, Mary's Dairy, Cones, and rapidly expanding chain Coldstone Creamery.

If you're strolling Nolita and your stomach gets grumbling, try Rice for something quick, cheap, and healthy, followed by the delightful gelato found at Ciao Bella – both on Mott Street. Chelsea? The Chelsea Market on Ninth Avenue at 16th Street features a superb little stroll where great soups, brownies, fruit, sandwiches, and such can be picked up along the way. West Village? We love the fish and chips of A Salt & Battery on Greenwich Avenue, cannoli from Rocco's Pastry Shop, and the decadent, cheap burgers of Corner Bistro. For a real treat, head to Two Little Red Hens on the Upper East Side – Second Avenue at 86th Street, to be precise – and pick up some world class

scones, muffins, or a slice of unforgettable fruit pie. Soutine Bakery on West 70th Street and the Popover Café on Amsterdam Avenue satiate choosy Upper West Siders, while Flatiron District fixtures City Bakery, 71 Irving, and the Shake Shack (luring long lines in Madison Square Park) are all chic, sweet retreats. Then, of course, there's the food court and market at Grand Central – the idea of which would have sent gourmands screaming just a few years ago, yet has proven to be a delicious, distinctively Manhattan experience.

If it's caffeine you need, caffeine you will find – and not only at Starbucks (though they continue to pop up everywhere). Since New Yorkers are constantly on the street, you can see evidence every morning – clutched in pedestrians' hands – how coffee, lattes, Mochaccinos, and such provide the real fuel that keeps the city's pistons pumping. There are mom and pop coffee shop all over the place, and our favorite is Joe on Waverly Place in the West Village. Beyond that? We have restaurants that serve only macaroni and cheese (S'mac on East 12th Street), risotto (Risotteria on Bleecker Street), or peanut butter sandwiches (Peanut Butter Co. on Sullivan Street). You can get Belgian frites with fancy dips, burgers, shakes, cupcakes, corn-on-the-cob, burritos, muffins…. It's making us hungry just thinking about it.

202 Café, Chelsea Market, 75 Ninth Avenue (W 16th St), Chelsea
Tel: 646 638 1173
Open: 8.30am–11.30pm Mon–Fri; 10am–11pm Sat/Sun

Located within the Chelsea Market – one of downtown's most stimulating little shopping areas, with its fish stores, bakeries, Italian dry goods shops, and butchers – is this sexy clothing and homewares shop/schmoozey eatery from designer-restaurateur Nicole Farhi (long a champion of melding high

design with good gastronomy at her uptown fashion emporium Nicole's). 202 Café draws a chic lot – publicists and editors, well-heeled Meatpacking District shoppers, the occasional sexy mommy – who come as much for the adorable atmosphere (communal tables; great, open-window views onto Ninth Avenue) as for the tasty fish with cilantro, chili, and lime; authentic fish and chips with mushy peas, or the warm goat cheese salad with prosciutto, figs, and pistachios. FYI, the waiters are not hard to look at, either.

Bouchon Bakery, Time Warner Center, 10 Columbus Circle (8th Ave), Upper West Side
Tel: 212 823 9366
Open: 8am–9pm Mon–Fri; 10am–9pm Sat; 10am–7pm Sun

Stand-out chef Thomas Keller – he of California's famed French Laundry and Bouchon, as well as Per Se upstairs at the Time Warner Center – does his best to appeal to the everyman with his handsome, approachable café that

features everything from CB&Js (cashew butter and apricot jam on toasted *brioche*, of course), ham and cheeses (*Madrange* ham and *Emmenthal* cheese on a baguette, to be precise), pâtes, and salads such as a flavorful one with chicken breast and romaine hearts, drizzled with creamy Parmesan dressing and flecked with shaved Botarga cheese. Humbly priced, given the huge talent behind it all, Bouchon Bakery is a prime choice for lunch, and a great place to pop in for a snack (perhaps the home-made Nutter Butters?) between luxury spending sprees at the rest of the TWC.

Burger Joint, Le Parker Meridien, 118 West 57th Street (6th Ave), Midtown West
Tel: 212 245 5000 www.parkermeridien.com
Open: daily, 11am–11.30pm (midnight Fri/Sat)

A spectacularly faithful rendition of a greasy spoon in a decidedly un-greasy

high-end hotel, Burger Joint offers Midtown burger enthusiasts a truly fine patty at under $7, in an environment that says "Don't even think of dragging that attitude in here." The danger, of course, is that it's an ironic statement; that having something

"low brow" in a ritzy place is somehow quirky and hilarious. But the reason it works is because it does not, in fact, work that angle – hallelujah. Roll up your sleeves, and if you're hankering for a stellar burger piled with cheese lettuce, pickles, onions with a milk shake, some Sam Adams on tap, and perhaps a whole dill pickle, you've got the right place. Also at Le Parker Meridien, Norma's, an all-breakfast knockout, featuring, among plenty of other delights, a Zillion Dollar lobster frittata with Sevruga caviar.

Café Gitane, 242 Mott Street (Prince), Nolita
Tel: 212 334 9552
Open: daily, 9am–midnight (12.30am Fri/Sat)

When you absolutely must be surrounded by French models, photographers, gallery owners, assorted other artsy types, and the people who love them, head to this sweet – if not self-aware – café on the trendy precipice between Soho and Nolita, where crusty baguettes, waitresses in mod outfits, and a decent offering of baked eggs await to tolerate you. While it's fun

to settle in among the fashionista throngs, you can take comfort from the fact that they are here mainly because of Café Gitane's convenient location. If you happen upon it later in the day, its Moroccan couscous with chicken, raisins, and eggplant is rather flavorful, and the salmon pot pie is both tasty and adorable. But go for breakfast – and not on a weekend – if you really want to experience its charms, unadulterated.

Caracas Arepa Bar, 93 East 7th Street (1st Ave), East Village
Tel: 212 529 2314 www.caracasarepabar.com
Open: daily, noon–10.45pm (9.45pm Sun)

Adorable, yet all business, the all-Venezuelan staff at this wildly popular East Village eatery will have you seated and smiling as soon as humanly possibly (though you may have to contend with a hip little contingent crowding the sidewalk outside, so get your name on the list quick). The *arepas*, delicious

corn *tortillas* stuffed with meats, beans, cheese, plantains, and such, are addictive, so be careful, start with two, and perhaps some fried plantains – dusted with salty cheese – to share for two. Particularly delicious are *De Pabellon* (shredded meat and black beans with plantains and aged cheese) and *La Playera* (shredded white fish with onions, garlic, and herbs); although everything is rather wonderful. There are also *empanadas*, nightly specials offerings, and knock-out fresh juices – passionfruit, and a not-too-sweet blackberry-strawberry combo.

Casa Mono, 52 Irving Place (E 17th St), Gramercy Park
Tel: 212 253 2773
Open: daily, noon–midnight

From Molto Mario and his clever team comes this pint-sized spot for relaxed Spanish-themed supping, right next door to the lovable Bar Jamon – yes, "ham bar" – that lives up to its name. Casa Mono is hard to argue with however you approach it, be it with glasses of beer alongside fennel-decked sweetbreads, fried duck egg and quail with figs, or a spot of any of the superbly selected Spanish wines alongside venison with butternut squash. It is best to try for a rejuvenating midday bite, because even if you do get a

table in the evening it is bound to be elbow-to-elbow with stuffy, foodie types who will ooh and ahh too loudly for you to properly enjoy yourself.

Chikalicious, 203 East 10th Street, East Village
Tel: 212-995-9511 www.chikalicious.com
Open: 3pm–5pm, 7pm–10:45pm Wed–Fri; 3pm–10:45pm Sat–Sun

Proving that the best desserts come from small storefronts, this diminutive East Village den of high-end sweet stuff is endlessly popular – hence the nightly lineup of sugar junkies waiting their turn outside. Tasteful twosome Don and Chika Tillman opened the Chik in 2003 to rave reviews, offering

discerning palates a smart selection of confections, wines, cheeses, and dreamy dishes like Darjeeling panna cotta with peach sorbet and cherry soup with corn ice cream paired with warm cornmeal pound cake. Popular is the three-course prix fixe, interpreted here as American desserts with French presentation in Japanese portions. There are only 20 seats, so be prepared to wait your turn... but know that once you're inside the elegant, spare space, the aforementioned wait will instantly vanish from your conscience. Do peruse the spot-on selection of Champagne and dessert wine.

City Bakery, 3 West 18th Street (Union Square), Chelsea
Tel: 212 366 1414 www.thecitybakery.com
Open: 7.30am–7pm (6.30pm Sat); 9am–6pm Sun

This place has so much going for it, it's hard to know where to begin, but the daily-churned hot chocolate and home-made marshmallow cubes are a good place to start. Then, there's the diner counter, where sticky, multilay-

ered grilled cheeses and BLT get served up with generosity. There are the buffet offerings – everything from fried catfish to coconut dusted haricots verts to perfectly anchovy-flecked Caesar salads; the soup and macaroni bar, often featuring a world-class *tortilla* soup; then the knock-your-socks-off chocolate chip cookies, raspberry bran muffins, or peanut butter drop cookies. It's sophisticated snacking at its finest, which might explain why the crème de New York's downtown crème line its tables and upper mezzanine. Oh yes, perfect coffee, every time. And caramelized French toast! The list goes on…

Emack & Bolio's, multiple locations
www.emackandbolios.com

The affection for Emack & Bolio's runs deep throughout the city... 40-plus hormone-free, organic ice creams, plenty of diet-friendly alternatives, and specialty yogurts – not to mention a plethora of candies and cookie toppings, and waffle cones – bring out the kid in all of us. Among the clever flavors – including the luxurious Deep Purple Cow (raspberry ice cream with

dried blueberries and white and milk chocolate chips, ideally served under the warmth of a layer of hot fudge) and low fat key lime pie yogurt – is something for everyone, plus there is a wide variety of teas, chais, and coffee beverages. All in all, a delightful little stopover when a pick-me-up is needed.

Florent, 69 Gansevoort Street (Washington), Meatpacking District
Tel: 212 989 5779 www.restaurantflorent.com
Open: daily, 24 hours

Don't trip over a model, designer, or other assorted sexy person as you sidle into this cherished Meatpacking District diner – a neighborhood landmark from way back before the Sex & the City crowd started buying there (it was more of a "sex on the street-y" vibe back then). Endlessly affable, jubilant, and philanthropic owner Florent Morellet occasionally presides over the chic crowd – yet the whole staff does its best to keep the vibe welcoming and the energy up, even at off-hours. There are more upscale charcuterie offerings and cheese plates, but really, what you want most is to grab a late-night booth with friends or a stool at the bar with a book and order the

marvelous veggie burger, black forest ham-speckled mac and cheese, or
some fragrant steamed PEI mussels and stop caring who's sitting at the next
table.

Joe, 141 Waverly Place (MacDougal), West Village
Tel: 212 924 6750 www.joetheartofcoffee.com
Open: daily, 7am (8am Sat/Sun)–8pm

What very well might be the finest, most reverential coffee shop in
Manhattan, Joe – whose employees jump through hoops (i.e. specialty courses and testing) for months before they are able to tackle the La Marzocca
espresso machine, which requires just the right amount of torque, cajoling,
and love – draws a crowd passionate not only about their caffeine, but

about the
place itself. It is
the quintessen-
tial Village cof-
fee shop: well
lit; perfectly
situated on
Waverly and
Gay Streets;
pint-sized,
making those
who score a
table feel as if

they've won some victory. Of course, not everyone who shows up is so tweaked… it is a treat, however, to get a corner seat by the window with an oversized donut and a cappuccino – the one with the special heart-shaped foam – and luxuriously make your way through the Sunday *New York Times*.

Nespresso Boutique Bar, 761 Madison Avenue (E 66th St), Upper East Side
Tel: 800 562 1465 www.nespresso.com
Open: 8am–8pm Mon–Fri; 9am–7pm Sat/Sun

Super-sleek and rather European-feeling, this haute coffee house strikes quite a contrast with the barista-driven downtown coffee emporiums where alterna-kids bang out their espresso molds to fashion together what hopefully becomes a semi-decent cup of Joe. Nespresso crafts its selections of

sealed coffee blends and uses its machines to remove the risk of human error and deliver precision cappuccinos, alongside a decent collection of pastries and desserts. While some might say this takes out a lot of the fun of having a favorite coffee house, others say 'perfect coffee is precise coffee'. If you prescribe to the latter camp, head on up to Madison and 66th.

Rice to Riches, 37 Spring Street (Mott), Nolita
Tel: 212 274 0008 www.ricetoriches.com
Open: daily, 11am–11pm (1am Fri/Sat)

What first seemed like a novelty that would disappear once the gimmick

died down has become a true mainstay of Nolita shopping culture. Although it's garish-looking (on otherwise trendy Spring Street), this futuristic mall-like rice pudding emporium is rather addictive, with flavors ranging from the traditional vanilla and strawberry to Hazelnut Chocolate Bear Hug, Surrender to Mango with lime, and Endangered Maple with sun-dried blue-berries. Decadent toppings such as caramel vanilla sauce and chilled espresso with cocoa are also available. Oh yes, you can order in bulk, and ship to nearly anywhere in the world. It would be nice if they used less plastic, or at least had container recycling, but perhaps that is in the works.

Rickshaw Dumpling Bar, 61 West 23rd Street (6th Ave), Chelsea
Tel: 212 741 7971 www.rickshawdumplings.com
Open: daily, 11.30am–9.30pm (8.30pm Sun)

Although it's cramped, this adorable, globe-lit dumpling emporium from

celebrated chef Anita Lo, of global-fusion standout Annisa, is perennially popular simply because these marvelously rendered steamed, fried, or soup-submerged dumplings are too good to be true. While waiting for your order or vying for a table, watch through the glass-encased kitchen as these heavenly little pockets are stuffed with everything from Peking duck, cabbage, scallions and Szechuan chicken, chili, and white soy beans to melted Callebaut chocolate for dessert (in a *wasabi mochi* wrapper). It is hard to grab a seat, so consider grabbing your dumplings to go and devouring them on a bench in nearby Madison Square Park.

Room 4 Dessert, 17 Cleveland Street (Kenmare), Nolita
Tel: 212 941 5405
Open: daily, 8am–midnight (1am Fri/Sat)

This is one high-end concept that cultivated foodies truly hope will stick. In south Nolita, this long, narrow space is the playground of notable pastry chef Will Goldfarb, a reverential confectioner who presents his delightful baked bites, gelatos, crumbles, cobblers, and such in themed tastings of four,

alongside dreamy gourmet teas or well-selected dessert wines. Cheese plates, drinkable confections, and whimsical candy *petit-fours* round out the menu of sugar-shocked end notes that have become the delight of monied downtown families and their youngsters as well as late-night hipsters who would rather end their evenings with a sugar rush than in a stupor. The staff is very knowledgeable about their product and the city food scene in general; it's a great place to unwind.

Shake Shack, Madison Square Park (E 24th St), Flatiron
Tel: 212 889 6600
Open: daily, 11am–11pm (April to November only)

Forget the darling buds of May... for many New Yorkers, the arrival of
spring is announced when the line in Madison Square Park starts curling in
on itself, as local business folk, high-priced nannies with privileged tots, personal assistants of uptown big wigs (sent there by personal drivers), and

such allow their stomachs to growl in anticipation for Shake Shack's bounty.
Restaurateur Danny Meyer struck it big with this concept – heaven-sent
burgers with haute trimmings; piled-high hot dogs; darn good fries; a nice
selection of shakes, frozen yogurt, and beer, all available within the green
confines of this nicely situated park at 23rd Street, between Madison Avenue
and the intersection of Broadway and Fifth. The lines have become hella-
cious, but just give yourself some time or go late; and be prepared to get
hooked.

The Tasting Room, 72 East 1st Street (1st Ave), East Village
Tel: 212 358 7831   www.thetastingroomnyc.com
Open: daily, 3pm–1am

While owners of this enthusiastically received tapas-style spot, Colin and
Rene Alevras, have since opened a larger spot with a full bar on Elizabeth
Street in Nolita and gone for larger course portions, this pint-sized original
space remains open as a café and wine bar, serving small tastes of clean, rus-
tic-inspired fare, alongside a well-chosen, primarily American wine list.
Specials change daily and are chalked on the wall, driven by market-fresh

143

tastes, and the grub tends to take its cues from pub fare, (a trend the city has absolutely come to embrace over the past few years, thanks to The Spotted Pig and newcomers such as the East Village's very promising European Union (E.U.). It's a sophisticated escape on a raucous downtown corner, and very much worth keeping on your radar.

Westville, 210 West 10th Street (Bleecker), West Village
Tel: 212 741 7971
Open: daily, 11.30am (10am Sat/Sun)–midnight

Mid-afternoon, when there's no line and the smiling waiters take the time to joke with you and cosset you, is the best time to come to this market-driven café on tree-lined West 10th Street, where the specials on chalk-boards include a vast selection of healthy greens. The kettle-cooked turkey burger is among the best in the city, the salads are generous and overflow-

ing, and the Americana classics — warm cobbler, corn on the cob, franks done up with gourmet condiments — stifle your hunger nicely so you're left to further shop your way through the West Village, free from stomach-grumbling in the Marc Jacobs changing room.

Wichcraft, multiple locations
www.wichcraftnyc.com

Be it for strong, marvelous coffee and a perfectly sized, salty-sweet scone in the morning; a well-priced, sophisticated sandwich or soup with long, crusty breadsticks for lunch; or an afternoon treat of not-too-sugary creamwich cookies and tea in the afternoon, 'Wichcraft, the winningly wonderful chain

of snack and sandwich shops from chef and TV's *Top Chef* judge Tom Colicchio (Craft, Craftsteak, Craftbar, Hearth) never fails to satisfy. Colicchio knows how to present simple concepts to sophisticated palates, and with these sandwich emporiums, he presents himself at his most approachable. Do try the fried egg, frisee, and gorgonzola sandwich... which feels particularly indulgent as a midday snack.

party...

If you want to get wild, lose yourself in a crowd, and give in to the possibility that anyone might spot you across a crowded room (or perhaps your spouse might just follow you through the flesh-packed throngs) and take you for a magical spin around the technicolor dance-floor, then New York is very much your city. Clubs big and small offer an array of opportunities to shake your groove thing. The thing is, what's hot one week can be deliriously dull the next. Here, we offer you a handful of venues that have proven decadent and escapist on multiple occasions. But we also suggest hitting up your concierge or local pals for suggestions when you land in town…. One day's pleasure cruise is the next day's Titanic.

Sure, times have certainly changed in the world of New York nightlife. As the population and per capita income of Manhattan residents have morphed, so too have the scenes, the venues, and the laws. Up until the late 1990s, New York was a place where partygoers of all stripes — straight, gay, cool, cheese-y, trendy, revolutionary, successful, broke, young, and old — could find their groove, and consequently get their groove on. Megaclubs like the Palladium, Sound Factory, Twilo, the Tunnel, and Limelight offered decadent playgrounds within which anyone — Joe Schmo or Joe Millionaire, alike — could lose themselves to the collective conscious. Then came a series of clubland scandals,

including the arrest of club czar (and consequent drug kingpin) Peter Gatien, and the 'Club Kids' murder of Angel Melendez by notorious party boy Michael Alig. The party soon felt like it was over, so over, especially when Mayor Rudy Giuliani revived a set of draconian cabaret laws that threatened to arrest revelers attempting to move rhythmically in bars without specific cabaret licenses. Thankfully, Mayor Bloomberg is not so wickedly opposed to 'social dance', and there are motions in local court advocating the right of New York's tail feather-shakers.

But don't let this back story give you the wrong impression. We New Yorkers can party harder than anyone, when we feel inclined, which is one of the multiple reasons many of us decide we can't live anywhere but here. Take, for example, the beautiful people who stroll in and stumble out of hotspots like the Plumm, Cielo, and the Pink Elephant. Scope out the hunky gay crowds at Mr. Black on Fridays, Element on Saturdays, or Hiro Ballroom at the Maritime Hotel on Sundays. Be bold and brazen and hop on over to Williamsburg for a rousing evening of sweaty, drunken dancing at Bembe, Warsaw, Black Betty, or Club Exit. Or go for the Ibiza uberclub experience at Midtowner Pacha.

In addition to places where you, yourself, can dance, we've included a batch of locales where extremely gorgeous, barely dressed women will dance for you. Yes, strip clubs... Fun stuff. Aside from being very naked, New York strippers are very hardworking, so stuff your pockets with plenty of cash – American money, please... Don't make the gals convert currency. Our choices are of the more upscale sort, but you can find seedier joints if you're in the market for that.... Others worth your dollar bills: FlashDancers on Broadway between 52nd and 53rd Streets, the Penthouse Executive Club on West 45th Street, and New York Dolls on Murray Street in the Financial District. We've said it before and we'll say it again: Look... Drool even... but don't touch.

APT, 419 West 13th Street (Washington), Meatpacking District
Tel: 212 414 4245   www.aptwebsite.com
Open: daily, 7pm–4am

As with most dance-y singles scenes you wander into, the crowd at APT really hinges on what night you hit it, but the environment is a real kicker and worth seeing. It's a two-story loft, hidden behind a pair of nondescript apartment doors on West 13th Street (worry not, you will find it), that's decorated like a maddeningly effective bachelor pad – complete with a bed,

a room-long end table, and personal artifacts from the fictional resident. Dancing takes place downstairs, and the DJ lineup – dotted with the finest in electronic and occasionally hip-hop – is truly compelling. Be warned: your cell phone won't work unless you're on the upstairs balcony, so prepare to be out of contact and just lose your head with the friends you're already with.

Bembe, 81 South 6th Street (Berry), Brooklyn
Tel: 718 387 5389   www.bembe.us
Open: daily, 7.30pm–4am

Williamsburg, Brooklyn has its fair share of destination nightspots – everything from the Brooklyn Ale House to Black Betty to Royal Oak to live music venues Galapagos and Pete's Candy Store. But Bembe, while blending in nicely, is one of the rare venues that could exist and thrive on the island of Manhattan, thanks to its sophisticated island cocktail menu, knowing staff

of sexy folk, and lively, salsa-driven dance-floor that gets shakers of all sorts moving to its addictive beat. As the room gets more crowded – and more and more fresh fruit cocktails circulate through your body – the music becomes all the more intense and compelling, thanks to adept DJs and a bass-friendly sound system. When all the shimmying become too much, take a load off in the hammock decadently strung in full view of the first-floor entranceway.

Black Betty, 366 Metropolitan Avenue (Havemeyer), Williamsburg, Brooklyn
Tel: 718 599 0243 www.blackbetty.net
Open: daily, 6pm–4am

For an attitude-free evening of carrying on, dancing with abandon, and cheap beverages, Black Betty beckons you across the bridge to Williamsburg and

into its sexy, anything-could-happen, bordello-esque environs. The eclectic music selection comes in three varieties: jukebox eclectic; addictive, booty-beckoning DJ sets; and loud, hyperactive live stuff. The crowd – like a dirty shaken Martini – gives a swift kick to your boredom, as hip young things of all sorts love to pay Miss Betty a visit, save perhaps the tube-top/shiny shirt set. If all the smooth movement gets your appetite up, or the heat gets too much on the tiny dance-floor, the adjoining Moroccan dining room – offering everything from falafel to couscous to tagines – will drop a taste bomb on you and get you primed for more. It gets packed on weekends, and the patrons tend to skew young – two elements that might attract or repel you, depending on how you roll.

BLVD and Crash Mansion @ BLVD, 199 Bowery (Spring), Lower East Side
Tel: 212 982 0740 www.blvdnyc.com
Open: 10pm–4am. Closed Sundays.

OK, fair warning: This 18,000-square-foot nightclub/lounge/restaurant is known for its less-than-charming door staff, outrageous prices, and occa-

sional occupation by the Bridge-and-Tunnel crowd. Still, it can be the site of some serious abandon. There's a bi-level dance area offering dramatic lighting and a 10,000 watt, state-of-the-art sound system; a slinky lounge area called Ultra with leather banquettes, plasma screens, and long, sloping bar of glazed oak; a hoity-toity VIP area called Pink; and the adjoining live music venue Crash Mansion, a slick spot to take in an intimate show or attend a

CD release party. The airy café provides a stark contrast to the hard-partying madness, with nice, eclectic fare with an Ecaudorian spin from executive chef Humberto Guallupa. If you can get past the elitism at the door and adequately prepare yourself for the end-of-the-night tally, you are in for a great time.

The Box, 189 Chrystie Street (Stanton), Lower East Side
Tel: 212 982 9301 www.theboxnyc.com
Open: daily, 10pm–2am (4am Weds–Sat)

Luring a frothy mix of Manhattan's chic set – not to mention a host of celebs and rock stars – with its lush, vaudevillian charms, this long-abandoned sign factory has sprung into new life with the help of nightlife star Serge Becker and a theatrical crew of investors that includes Simon

Hammerstein, the grandson of theater legend Oscar Hammerstein. The result: an energetic, sexy bi-level space – complete with a stage door that opens onto trendy Freeman Alley – that's dedicated to posh dining and old-school entertainment like Follies-style dancers, balladeers, circus performances, and 'oddities'. Of course, it's basically a throwback supper club sporting some newfangled hooks – namely top-tier DJs and a menu of contemporary bites. But mainly it will be remembered as a decadent homage to the past, right down to the warn layers of wallpaper.

China 1 and Antique Lounge, 50 Avenue B (E 4th St), East Village
Tel: 212 375 0665 www.china1nyc.com
Open: 6pm (4pm Sun)–2am (4am Fri/Sat). Closed Mondays.

An infectious feeling of fun pours from its street-level bar onto the sidewalk at this increasingly popular Alphabet City lounge-nightspot-restaurant. Formerly called No. 1 Chinese, the deceptively cavernous, bi-level space offers diners upscale takes on traditional Chinese take-out faves, tipplers a fine menu of specialty cocktails that includes a tiramisu shooter and a dreamy cucumber saketini, and partiers a stylishly appointed playground in

which to flirt, schmooze, and work up a sweat with their favorite, best-rehearsed dance moves. The basement lounge – which fits up to 200 heat-seekers – offers an appealing, retro mix of Chinese antiques (think: lanterns, opium beds, Buddhas) as well as an intricate aquarium and a sumptuous deep-red lighting scheme. With live jazz sets and skilled DJs taking the crowd's temperature all weekend, it's a stylish, sexy affair across the board. No wonder the hottest bands and young celebs in from the west coast flock to it in droves.

Cielo, 18 Little West 12th Street (9th Ave), Meatpacking District
Tel: 212 645 5700 www.cieloclub.com
Open: 9.30pm–3.30am Mon; 10.30pm–4am Weds; 11pm–4am Thurs–Sat; 10pm–4am Sun. Closed Tuesdays.

Be thick-skinned if the doormen give you grief outside this exclusive downtown mini-club. They're paid to be selective, and that attitude they give off inspires more nostalgia than anything else. Once inside, you'll melt into the slick grooves of an international roster of house music DJs and mingle among plenty of body-baring beauties and guys who love to flash their plastic. Touting an indelible Ibiza vibe, this banquette-lined venue – complete with padded walls so you can sink deep into a kiss or stumble without wrecking yourself – will scratch your booty-shaking itch (not to mention empty your wallet: bottle service is the way it's done in this set, if you decide to sit). When you're all sweaty and bleary-eyed, stop in at Florent on Gansevoort Street for some rejuvenating grub before you conk out.

D'Or, West 55th Street (8th Ave), Midtown West
Tel: 212 245 7715
Open: 6pm–2am (4am Thurs–Sat). Closed Sundays.

From jet-setting hotelier Vikram Chatwal and lounge master Greg Brier

comes a glitzy Midtown lounge with a decidedly downtown feel. Revelers enter through new eatery Amalia, down a flashy, illuminated staircase of mosaic tiles and into a subterranean cavern with exposed brick and brown leather banquettes, and gilded mirrors. Its fantastical crystal chandelier and gold-front bar – not to mention a well-manned DJ booth with a banging sound system and an alt-wait staff that must have been imported from a lower zip code – give the space some street cred its fellow neighborhood lounges lack. You'll notice that D'Or is the lowest level of Chatwal's decadent Dream Hotel (see Sleep), a boutique traveler's treat... do yourself a favor and check out the lobby's mesmerizing fish tanks when you've got a buzz on.

Element, 225 East Houston Street (Essex), Lower East Side
Tel: 212 254 2200 www.elementny.com
Open: 10pm–4am Thurs–Sun

Aged Goth kids affectionately remember this space as the Bank – an actual former bank on the Lower East Side which served as a longtime haven for creatures of the night in Siouxsie and the Banshees eyeliner and torn fishnets. (Where have they all gone? They are missed.) After playing host to a number of failed ventures, the grand space is hitting its stride again as

Element, with its eclectic weekly parties (including a peppy gay party on Saturday nights), mazelike brick basement, and high mezzanine overlooking the expansive dance-floor. It's the closest thing to the early 1990s we can find, combining the virtues of size, eclecticism, superb sound, and enough surprises to keep even jaded after-darkers coming back. It's all about good energy, people!

Hiro Ballroom, The Maritime Hotel, 371 West 16th Street (9th Ave), Chelsea
Tel: 212 727 0212 www.themaritimehotel.com
Open: 10pm–4am Thurs–Sun

If you've got a cool outfit to show off – a chic, futuristic gown or new Adidas track suit, perhaps? – it will undoubtedly look awesome against this eccentric Japanese-themed backdrop right out of *Kill Bill 1* (or, of course, the kung-fu movies it tried to emulate). The dance-floor gets jumping most nights by midnight, while the banquette areas make well-heeled revelers feel

like VIPs every time. A 20-foot vaulted barrel ceiling, paper lanterns, and an expansive bar area make for a visual treat you won't soon forget, while the beats – fun, contemporary fare that inspire a fair share of bon-bon shaking – are first-class all the way.

Marquee, 289 Tenth Avenue (W 26th St), Chelsea
Tel: 646 473 0202 www.marqueeny.com
Open: 10pm–4am. Closed Sundays and Mondays.

Self-dubbed an "ultralounge," this much-loved, much-despised bi-level jet-set nightclub has undeniable sex appeal, and has hosted the biggest celebs from the worlds of fashion, film, music, and society throughout the years. What this means for you: a sizeable wait at the door (unless you've slept with the right person beforehand) and a host of stylish ways to while away the hours once inside. Owners Jason Strauss and Noah Tepperberg have long found success whipping up star-studded soirees in the glitzy vacation area of the

155

Hamptons, and this space – open since 2003 – has managed to lap its neigh-boring nightspots in terms of popularity. Why? Three interconnecting areas of schmoozing, serenaded by world-class DJ selections via a top-notch sound system, and, of course, models scattered about. Though located in North Chelsea, and area quickly becoming thought of as "so last year," Marquee stands a good chance of sticking around for a long while.

Mr. Black, 643 Broadway (Bleecker), East Village
Tel: 212 253 2560
Open: 10pm–6am (4am Weds/Thurs). Closed Mondays.

Over the last decade, few gay spots have managed to create a sexy, surpris-ing mix of clientele and keep the momentum going. But Mr. Black started out strong and flew under the radar long enough to build up a serious buzz... plus nobody saw it coming. Its location on Broadway and Bleecker

(so often the gays are sequestered to Alphabet City or Chelsea) seemed so… accepting! Yet its dim, sexy, underground allure and wicked DJ sessions seemed so… naughty! The eye-candy bartenders are straight half the time, but they've got no problem flirting with the handsome clientele, while the lean, scruffy go-go dancers defy the traditional beefcake stereotype. The DJs are top notch, and the party promoters know how to work that cabaret license. Best of all: you don't need to be gay to enjoy yourself.

Pacha NYC, 618 W 46th Street (11th Ave), Hell's Kitchen
Tel: 212 209 7500 www.pachanyc.com
Open: 5pm–4am Thurs; 10pm–6am Fri–Sat

We all like to fancy ourselves worthy of the grandest treatment available. Whether that is true or not is impossible to say. But at Pacha NYC – the Manhattan outpost of the international nightclub/jet-set-lifestyle-location brand – mere mortals can get lost in the decadent good life for at least one

evening. A megaclub in post-megaclub New York City (oh, how we miss the Palladium, Twilo, and Sound Factory – the space's former incarnation), Pacha NYC trades on the sexy vibe imported from its seasonal flagship location in Ibiza, Spain – which is reinforced by its 24 other international outposts – and manages to deliver a unique strain of hyperactive pleasure to the throngs of electronic music fans who flock in – The T.G.I. Fridays of night-clubs, this is not. Over 2,700 people fit in the 30,000 square foot, five-floor space – tricked out with curved seating alcoves; smooth, multicolored light-ing; projections; a custom wooden dance-floor; a dramatic staircase; an atri-um level; and an exclusive VIP floor – so be prepared to sacrifice personal space for DJ/co-owner Erick Morillo's transporting tunes.

Pink Elephant, 527 West 27th Street (10th Ave), Chelsea
Tel: 212 463 0000   www.pinkelephantclub.com
Open: 11pm–4am Weds–Sat

If world-class house music's your thing, and you've got money to spend, then get thee to the Pink Elephant, a supersexy destination – formerly in the Meatpacking District, now transplanted to Upper Chelsea – where a floating glass-tile bar, a sunken dance-floor, curved lounge areas, and deep red hue get a well-heeled crowd in the mood for serious abandon (hopefully not the reckless kind). There are also crystal chandeliers and an enjoyable foliage

theme, with plant-lined staircases and such. The crowd, despite a few unavoidable dips and drips, tends to be rather chic and sexy, and that bottle service concept – tedious to some at this point – is alive and well.

The Plumm, 246 West 14th Street (7th Ave), West Village
Tel: 212 675 1567   www.theplumm.com
Open: daily, 10pm–4am

To some, it's a sleek sexy retreat where the high-powered elite meet, mingle, and pair off. To others, it's a nightmarish scene where scantily clad PR assistants throw themselves shamelessly at sons of the C-List. We say: try anything once…You can decide for yourself. Chances are you'll get a kick out of the gals dancing on the banquettes and the slick-dressed guys looking to score. Keep in mind that the subterranean lounge makes a nice escape when the crowd gets too raucous. Owned by impresario Noel Ashman and a host of random celebrities like Damon Dash and Simon Rex, it definitely

gets boldfacers ordering off its bottle service menu here and there, and European DJs do a good job of keeping you grooving.

STRIP CLUBS

Larry Flynt's Hustler Club, 641 West 51st Street (11th Ave), Midtown West
Tel: 212 247 2460
Open: daily, 6pm (8pm Sat/Sun)–4am (2am Sun)

It's decadence and big bucks galore at Hustler magnate Larry Flynt's Manhattan dude fantasy outpost. Located on the West Side Highway, the Hustler Club features a sizable roster of high-class honies shaking what their (horrified?) mothers gave them. A natural choice for Platinum Card-carrying suits, bad-boy celebrities, in-town athletes, and bachelor parties, it has table dances, private "fantasy rooms" for up-close milkshakes, Champagne rooms, bottle service, and specialty cocktails. Don't expect to see the full Monty, people… this is a topless spot, and the va-jayjays are staying artfully concealed. But with all the rhythmic shaking and aggressive pandering to the male ego, you won't miss a thing. A word of caution: don't touch them unless you want a really bad ending to your day.

Scores, 333 East 60th Street (2nd Ave), Upper East Side
Tel: 212 421 3600 www.scoresny.com
Open: daily, 7pm–4am (2am Sun)

The mother of all NYC strip clubs, Scores features cream of the crop exotic dancers – the kind you'd pant over even if you didn't know about their secret birthmarks. Tall, busty, and talented at strutting in heels, these ladies know how to work the sweat onto your brows and the money out of your wallets. It's a fave of all sorts of boldfacers, who undoubtedly have their favorite "Dream Girl" all picked out. (That's how they're known, people.) Further delighting the decadent alpha male, it's a tobacco bar, and a top-notch selection of cigars is available. All this, plus the requisite private dances, make for a spicy evening, indeed.

Ten's World Class Cabaret, 35 East 21st Street (Broadway), Flatiron District
Tel: 212 254 2444
Open: 6pm (8pm Mon, Sat)–4am. Closed Sundays.

Located ever so conveniently around the corner from half of the good furniture stores in town, libidinous lads are more than glad to take a seat at this dignified titty bar, where a nice cross-section of beauties make visitors feel very welcome before hypnotizing them with the pendulous motion of their breasts. It's nice to see a change from the traditional Barbie up there, and the decently prepared menu of "rich dude food" ensures that your stomach won't growl while you're receiving your third or fourth lap dance. (How embarrassing!) We like these girls, so don't try and fondle them or treat them like meat. They're paying their way through college, after all. Plus, you'll be thrown out on your ass.

COMEDY CLUBS

Caroline's Comedy Club, 1626 Broadway (W 50th St), Midtown West
Tel: 212 757 4100 www.carolines.com
Open: 5.30–11pm (2am Fri/Sat)

Welcoming top names from all corners of the comedy industry, this Times Square mainstay, here since 1992, has acts seven nights a week.

Comedy Cellar, 117 MacDougal Street (Minetta), West Village

Tel: 212 254 3480   www.comedycellar.com
Show times: 9pm & 11pm Sun–Thurs; 8pm, 9.45pm & 11.30pm Fri; 7.30pm, 9.15pm, 11pm and 12.45am Sat

A subterranean club right off the NYU campus, where recognizable up-and-comers (and occasional big names) yuk it up in an intimate atmosphere – after working the sidewalk to lure passers-by inside.

Comic Strip Live, 1568 Second Avenue (E 81st St), Upper East Side

Tel: 212 861 9386   www.comicstriplive.com
Open: 8.30pm (8pm Sat/Sun)–11.30pm (12.30am Fri, 2am Sat, 1.30am Sun)

This cramped, headshot-lined club, founded in 1975, is the legendary spot where many of comedy's biggest names got their start and worked the room – starting with Eddie Murphy and followed by Chris Rock, Paul Reiser, Adam Sandler, Judy Gold, Caroline Rhea, and Jerry Seinfeld. To this day, established acts welcome promising rosters of talent nightly, with benefits interspersed. Reservations are a must.

Gotham Comedy Club, 208 West 23rd Street (7th Ave), Chelsea

Tel: 212 367 9000   www.gothamcomedyclub.com
Shows: 8.30pm Sun–Thurs; 8.30pm & 10.30pm Fri; 8pm, 10pm & 11.45pm Sat

Located next to the Chelsea Hotel, this sizable, elegantly decorated space is arguably the ritziest stand-up spot in the city, with a fantastic roster of talent – from veterans to new talent. Two comedians opened it with the intention of interjecting a little polish to the dirty jokes industry; no wonder Seinfeld used it as the backdrop for his documentary, Comedian.

B.B. King Blues Club & Grill, 237 West 42nd Street (7th Ave), Midtown West
Tel: 212 997 4144   www.bbkingblues.com
Open: daily, 11am–1am

Smack-dab in the center of Times Square, this intimate venue – owned by the family behind downtown's famous Blue Note – draws world-class acts from both the jazz and pop worlds.

Blue Note, 131 West 3rd Street (MacDougal), West Village
Tel: 212 475 8592   www.bluenote.net
Open: daily, 6pm–1am (4am Fri/Sat)

The top draw of the downtown jazz clubs, this institution – which opened its doors in 1981 – regularly welcomes jazz giants such as Chick Corea, Cassandra Wilson, and Donald Harrison.

Bowery Ballroom, 6 Delancey Street (Bowery), Lower East Side
Tel: 212 533 2111   www.boweryballroom.com

A great-feeling space where mostly alternative bands play sell-out shows to appreciative hip crowds who know all the words to their songs. Take time to enjoy the subterranean bar.

Knitting Factory, 74 Leonard Street (Church), Financial District
Tel: 212 219 3055   www.knittingfactory.com
Open: daily, 5pm–4am

A great space for smaller shows, with a diverse cross-section of acts performing in three spaces. Don't miss the high-octane scene at hip-hop karaoke.

Riverside Church, 490 Riverside Drive (W 122nd St), Upper West Side
Tel: 212 870 6700 www.theriversidechurchny.org
Open: daily, 7am–10pm

This revered Gothic church – known for its hyper-involved and progressive interdenominational mission – hosts theater performances and otherworldly concerts from top names.

Webster Hall, 125 East 11th Street (4th Ave), East Village
Tel: 212 353 1600 www.websterhall.com
Open: 10pm–4am Thurs–Sat

While it's best known as an unchallenging nightclub, the Bowery Presents... series has given new life to its intimate rocker stage with performers such as Sonic Youth, Yo La Tengo, and Arcade Fire.

culture...

While all of the categories we are covering in this book have their undeniable virtues, this section is probably our favorite. This is New York, darlings… a city that runs on creativity and culture. For more than a century, New York has played home to groundbreaking cultural movements and influenced the world at large with its wildly creative constituents. Authors, painters, poets, musicians – their influence can be felt in every corner of Gotham. From the Harlem Renaissance and the beat poetry scene to punk music culture and the roots of modern dance – in the works of Dorthy Parker, James Baldwin, Walt Whitman – New York served as great artists' most poignant inspiration, and lives on as a monument to their significance.

Sure, Broadway's theaters and their big budget spectacles immediately leap to mind – *A Chorus Line*, *Hairspray*, *Spamalot*, *Spring Awakening*, and *The Phantom of the Opera* are yours for the viewing – and we suggest clicking on Broadway.com the second you start to plan your trip so you can snag seats to a top show. But that's not all, kids. Off-Broadway and Off-Off-Broadway shows are everywhere, and very worthy of being explored. We've described a few theaters, but that's just a small sampling of what you can find. We've got Lincoln Center and Carnegie Hall, where the finest operatic and classical music performers come to move you in high style. There are jazz clubs of all shapes and sizes, and concert venues of various sizes hosting everything from punk to folk to the biggest names in pop. The Riverside Church in Harlem is the site of diverse music and theatrical performances, with students from neighboring Columbia University frequently using the space to stage their latest offerings. You could easily wile away a few hours exploring the numerous tiny galleries dot West Chelsea, making the rounds at the Museum of Modern Art (right), or exploring Eastern works at the Rubin Museum of Art in Chelsea (Rmanyc.org). For kicks, we added some classic movie theaters – though please don't see too many while you're here. That's like ordering a hooker and playing Parcheesi with her.

Also included here is a short list of the city's most well known monuments. There are so many places to see, with so much history and significance to

them.... Make sure your cameras have batteries, please. That brings us to one of the city's most beloved monuments that is sadly no longer with us—the World Trade Center. Obviously, the Twin Towers that long stood on Lower West Manhattan were a proud symbol of America's financial strength, and an indelible source of distinction and pride to its citizens. The events of September 11, 2001, rocked this city to its core, and we miss our towers, not to mention our fellow New Yorkers who died that day, very much. But what happened in the days, months, and years following the terrorist attack was miraculous. New Yorkers – long thought of as gruff and unfriendly – came together for each other and for the city itself. 9-11 galvanized the city, proving that New Yorkers are unsinkable and stick together in a time of crisis. It was quite something. If you'd like to visit the site where the towers once stood – now under heavy construction – you can find it on Cortlandt Street (off of the Chambers Street subway stop).

OK, had to get that out. Now, get out there and partake of the city's cultural bounty.

MUSEUMS/GALLERIES

American Museum of Natural History/Hayden Planetarium, Central Park West at 79th Street, Upper West Side
Tel: 212 769 5100 www.amnh.org
Open: daily, 10am–5.45pm

You don't have to be a kid to love everything about this mammoth institution, founded in 1869 and relocated to its present site in 1874. With hall after hall, 45 in total, of natural artifacts – focusing on everything from human biology and evolution to African mammals, and including, of course, dinosaurs – there is something to fascinate everyone in your group (even architecture buffs, thanks to the diverse design elements of the complex's structure). In addition to the famous blue whale in the Hall of Ocean Life, the 600-plus dinosaur fossils, and rooms of ecosystem-themed taxidermy, visitors refuse to miss the Rose Center for Earth and Space – the marvelous glass structure that houses the mind-blowing Hayden Planetarium. The wildly popular exhibits focus on everything from exotic live butterflies to the roots of human origins to precious metals.

Brooklyn Museum of Art, 200 Eastern Parkway, Brooklyn
Tel: 718 638 5000 www.brooklynmuseum.org
Open: 10am–5pm Wed–Fri; 11am–6pm Sat–Sun

Known for its cutting-edge exhibitions (the photographer Annie Liebovitz, the sculptor Ron Mueck) and extensive collection of Egyptian art, this cavernous Beaux Arts space – open since 1897 – houses over one and a half million pieces, from ancient to contemporary. Located close to downtown Brooklyn, Prospect Park, and several vibrant neighborhoods including Fort Green, Park Slope, and Prospect Heights, it is well worth a trip out of Manhattan.

The Cloisters, 99 Margaret Corbin Drive, Washington Heights
Tel: 212 923 3700 www.metmuseum.org
Open: 9.30am–4.45pm (5.15pm Mar–Oct). Closed Mondays.

One of the most peaceful, rejuvenating places in all of New York City, the Cloisters – set within lovely Fort Tryon Park, with a dramatic view of the Hudson River – are a branch of the Metropolitan Museum of Art that features the art and architecture of medieval Europe. Featuring invaluable tapestries, serene gardens, stained glass, manuscripts, and more – plus guest lectures and guided tours – this is a divine way to get away from the city madness for an afternoon.

Cooper-Hewitt National Design Museum, 2 East 91st Street, Upper East Side
Tel: 212 849 8400   www.cooperhewitt.org
Open: 10am (noon Sun)–5pm (9pm Fri, 6pm Sat/Sun)

Located in Andrew Carnegie's transporting 64-room Upper East Side mansion, this institution – part of the Smithsonian Institute – celebrates classic and contemporary design and architecture, with an extensive collection of wall coverings, sketches, textiles, and objects that push the boundaries of product design and decorative art.

Deitch Projects, 76 Grand Street (Wooster), Lower East Side
Tel: 212 343 7300   www.deitch.com
Open: noon–6pm. Closed Sundays and Mondays.

This hip, renowned gallery founded by Jeffrey Deitch has presented over 120 solo exhibits since opening its doors in 1996, and invites art stars and emerging pioneers of the music, fashion, performance, and visual worlds to be bold within its halls.

The Frick Collection, 1 East 70th Street (5th Ave), Upper East Side
Tel: 212 288 0700   www.frick.org
Open: 10am–6pm Tues–Sat; 11am–5pm Sun

Major European masterworks (including Vermeers, Goyas, El Grecos, and Thomas Gainsboroughs), frescoes, 18th-century French furniture and porcelain, and Limoges enamels await your perusal in the former estate of ill-reputed steel tycoon Henry Clay Frick.

Lower Eastside Tenement Museum, 97 Orchard Street (Broome), Lower East Side

Tel: 212 431 0233 www.tenement.org
Open: check website for tour times

This fascinating trip back in time is all about immigrant roots, with five floors of apartments recreating daily life in the late 19th and early 20th centuries from different ethnic perspectives. You must take the guided tour to gain access – and you'll be glad you did. Aside from the treasures of the building itself, the Tenement Museum hosts walking tours around the neighborhood that shed interesting light on the much-gentrified surroundings.

Marlborough Gallery, 40 West 57th Street, second floor (5th Ave), Upper West Side

Tel: 212 541 4900 www.marlboroughgallery.com
Open: 10am–5.30pm. Closed Sundays.

A handsome, expansive gallery complete with a sculpture garden, this revered contemporary art dealer has London roots; the original Marlborough was founded in 1946 on Albemarle Street. This outpost regularly showcases solo exhibitions for big guns within its two galleries, including Tom Otterness, Hunt Slonem, and Richard Estes.

Metropolitan Museum of Art, 1000 Fifth Avenue (E 81st St), Upper East Side

Tel: 212 535 7710 www.metmuseum.org
Open: 9.30am–5.30pm (9pm Fri/Sat). Closed Mondays.

No city institution carries the cultural heft of the Met, located on the east side of Central Park at 82nd Street, with its 17 renowned curatorial departments and incredible temporary exhibitions that run the gamut from ancient and historic to cutting-edge contemporary. Everywhere you turn is something spectacular, be it the unparalleled Egyptian collection, the glitzy Costume Institute, the Asian and African art wings, the newly restored European sculpture department, the Islamic section, or the European art galleries featuring some of the most acclaimed pieces from the 12th through the 19th centuries. Sun worshipers can't get enough of the rooftop, where sandwiches and beverages are served against the glorious backdrop of Central Park.

Museum of Modern Art (MoMA), 11 West 53rd Street (5th Ave), Midtown West
Tel: 212 708 9400   www.moma.org
Open: 10.30am–5.30pm (8pm Fri). Closed Tuesdays.

Reimagined by Japanese architect Yoshio Taniguchi, the MoMA reopened to an impatient public in 2004 having been closed since May of 2002, offering its visitors over 150,000 diverse pieces of art as well as more than 22,000 films and four million film stills from a cross-section of media and world-class exhibitions. The museum was founded in 1929, with the mission of challenging the conventions of the museum world – and that it has, ever since.

Solomon R. Guggenheim Museum, 1071 Fifth Avenue (E 88th St), Upper East Side
Tel: 212 423 3500   www.guggenheim.org
Open: 10am–5.45pm (7.45pm Fri). Closed Thursdays.

The Guggenheim is truly a sight to behold, an iconic structure built by Frank Lloyd Wright in 1959 that, at the time, drew a line in the sand between old- and new-school architects. Now a revered city treasure, the Guggenheim houses important works from the 19th and 20th centuries – Picassos, Van Goghs, Chagalls, Kandinskys – and puts on wildly popular exhibits within its spiral hallways.

The Whitney Museum of American Art, 945 Madison Avenue (E 75th St), Upper East Side
Tel: 212 570 3676   www.whitney.org
Open: 11am (1pm Fri)–6pm (9pm Fri). Closed Mondays and Tuesdays.

Founded in 1931 from the personal collection of Gertrude Vanderbilt Whitney, the Whitney is dedicated to the celebration and preservation of contemporary American art, and is the top spot in town for masterworks of the 20th century. Boasting over 14,000 pieces (grown from its 700 original pieces, mostly donated by Ms. Whitney and augmented through the years by other esteemed donors), the Museum, designed by Marcel Breuer, is an exceptional structure, dramatically angled and crafted of glass and polished stone. The Whitney Biennial is a much-anticipated event each year, showcasing the best young artists, and temporary exhibitions are always an enormous, citywide draw.

Zach Feuer Gallery, 530 West 24th Street (10th Ave), Chelsea
Tel: 212 989 7700 www.zachfeuer.com
Open: 10am–6pm Tues–Sat

This 2,000-square-foot gallery space hosts stand-out artists from a wide cross-section of media: video installation, performance art, painting, photography, sculpture, and so on. Young powerhouse Feuer – whose LA gallery and new London gallery called Brown have earned him additional cred on the international art scene – knows how to pick the top young talent, as is evidenced by his continued support of artists such as painter-phenomenon Dana Schutz.

SIGHTSEEING

The Circle Line, Pier 83, West 42nd Street (12th Ave), Upper West Side
Tel: 212 563 3200 www.circleline.com

The city's go-to sightseeing cruises, with three-hour trips around Manhattan Island, two-hour half-island trips, dazzling evening cruises called "Harbor Lights," and special excursions out to Liberty Island for a close-up view of the Statue of Liberty. There are bevies, food, and tourist merchandise available on-board. For something a tad zippier, the loudly painted Beast speedboat takes travelers on a fast-paced trip through the harbor – at 45 mph to be exact – with a quick photo op stop at the Statue of Liberty.

Empire State Building, 350 Fifth Avenue (E 35th St), Murray Hill
Tel: 212 736 3100 www.esbnyc.com
Open: daily, 8am–midnight

The towering visual symbol of Manhattan stands 102 stories high on 34th Street and Fifth Avenue. An Art Deco triumph, and the highest building in the world for half of last century, the Empire State draws hefty crowds to its 86th-floor observation deck, where the view expands far beyond the city on clear days. Its colored lights give the city a lift every night, with special colors to commemorate certain holidays and special events. If the queues are too long head up to the Rockerfeller Centre for the "Top of the Rock" experience, the queues are shorter and the view equally stunning, and you get to see the Empire State Building.

Grand Central Terminal, Park Avenue (E 42nd St), Midtown East
Tel: 212 340 2210 www.grandcentralterminal.com

After a thorough refurbishment in the late 1990s, this classic Beaux Arts building – a bustling train hub that relentlessly shuffles commuters in and out of the tri-state area – serves as home to several great restaurants (Michael Jordon's The Steak House, Cipriani Dolci, and Metrazur), a high-end market, specialty shops, and the exquisite, clubby bar the Campbell Apartment. The common areas often host themed exhibits and cultural fairs, and the Tiffany blue-domed ceiling illustrates the constellations.

New York Public Library, Fifth Avenue (E 42nd St), Midtown West
Tel: 212 930 0830 www.nypl.org
Open: 11am–7.30pm Tues–Wed; 10am–6pm Thurs–Sat; 1–5pm Sun. Closed Mondays.

Nearly a century old (it opened in 1911), this grand library – guarded out front by the iconic lion sculptures Patience and Fortitude – is home to an unprecedented collection of important works and hosts exceptional art and history exhibits. Enormous and elegant, it's a veritable temple for book-worms, with frequent reading seminars and daily tours.

Rockefeller Center, Fifth and Sixth Avenue (W 49th St), Midtown West
www.rockefellercenter.com

A beloved promenade connecting Fifth and Sixth Avenues, Rock Center offers a great way to spend some time and is home to everything from Radio City Music Hall to the GE Building to NBC Studios and several fine dining establishments. (Del Frisco's steaks are amazing; tel: 212 575 5129.) Art and history tours are often guided by some of the most colorful characters in the city, and, yes, a gigantic Norway spruce becomes the Rockefeller Center Christmas Tree each year, presiding over Charlie Brown-esque ice-skaters. Shop anywhere from Banana Republic to Godiva to Swarovski, and finish up with a trip up to the marvelous Rainbow Room, on the 65th floor of 30 Rockefeller Plaza (tel: 212 632 5000).

Saint Patrick's Cathedral, Fifth Avenue (E 50th St) Midtown East
Tel: 212 753 2261   www.saintpatrickscathedral.org
Open: daily, 6.30am–8.45pm

This marvelous, intricate church – perhaps the most famous in the country – is the largest Gothic-style Catholic cathedral in the US. Built in 1858 to replace the original St. Patrick's – downtown in what is now Nolita – this grand house of worship can fit up to 2,200 people and reaches 405 feet above the street. It is said that over 3 million people enter through its doors each year (so come prepared to face a crowd).

South Street Seaport, 19 Fulton Street (Front), Financial District
Tel: 212 732 8257   www.southstreetseaport.com

This lively shopping, dining, and strolling enclave in the middle of the Financial District was the longtime port for Manhattan, and now invites shoppers, local businessmen, and tourists to its promenade, where a fantastic nautical museum, the South Street Seaport Museum, sits alongside popular shops such as Abercrombie & Fitch, Coach, and Victoria's Secret. The on-site restaurants and bars are a tad on the hokey side, but the spectacular view – right beneath the Brooklyn Bridge on the edge of the river – and neat sense of nautical history are why you go, anyway.

Staten Island Ferry, Whitehall Terminal, Whitehall Street (South), Battery Park
Tel: 718 815 BOAT www.siferry.com

Get something free for once, with this gratis ferry ride between Manhattan and Staten Island. Leaving every half hour, this beloved tub transports mass quantities of commuters, along with folks who just love the sea air and the view of the Statue of Liberty. Cheap beer and snacks are for sale down below.

The Statue of Liberty, Liberty Island
Tel: 212 269 5755 (ferry information) www.statueofliberty.org

Lady Liberty stands 305 feet tall and never fails to thrill. A gift from the French in the late 1800s, the statue was created to symbolize America's willingness to accept in the "huddled masses" and "wretched refuse" of the world, and remains to this day an emotional site for immigrants. Upper floors are no longer available to the public following September 11, but there is still plenty to see – plus the Statue of Liberty Museum and guided tours (tel: 866 782 8834).

United Nations, First Avenue (E 46th St), Upper East Side
Tel: 212 963 7113
Open: 9.30am–4.45pm Mon–Fri; 10am–4.30pm Sat/Sun

The United Nations member countries are represented along six blocks on the east side of the city, the world's epicenter of international relations. A tour through its halls, offered in over 20 languages, is downright enlightening. The bookstore offers official UN reports, as well as tourist paraphernalia.

OPERA, BALLET and DANCE

Brooklyn Academy of Music (BAM), 30 Lafayette Avenue, Brooklyn
Tel: 718 636 4100 www.bam.org

Groundbreaking, exhilarating performances – from the Mark Morris Dance Company and opera productions to a spectacular roster of music and the edgy theater pieces of top international directors – are the stock and trade of this revered Brooklyn-based cultural institution. The BAM Rose Cinemas host great film series and show genre-defying movies from the past and present.

City Center, 131 West 55th Street (5th Ave), Midtown West
Tel: 212 581 1212 www.nycitycenter.org

Opened in 1943, this vast, dramatic performance space plays host to the biggest names in dance – everything from the Kirov Ballet and American Ballet Theatre to the Alvin Ailey Dance Theater and the Paul Taylor Dance Company. It's also the home of the Manhattan Theater Club, and puts on a series called "Encores," restagings of lesser known musicals.

The Joyce Theater, 175 Eighth Avenue (W 19th), Chelsea
Tel: 212 691 9740 www.joyce.org

A dance institution founded in 1982, this progressive space offers enthusiasts of the art a spectacular roster of modern acts, with buzzworthy troupes from all over the world gracing its stage. Everything in this Chelsea-based, 472-seat theater is state-or-the-art (it was converted from a movie house), while three dance studios comprise a sister property, Joyce Soho (155 Mercer Street, Soho; tel: 212 431 9233).

Lincoln Center for the Performing Arts, Broadway (W62nd), Upper West Side
Tel: 212 875 5000 www.lincolncenter.org

The heartbeat of city culture, this splendid arts institution – resplendent with its public fountain and classic performance halls such as Alice Tully Hall and Avery Fisher Hall – offers the finest in live entertainment. Home to the New York City Opera, New York City Ballet, New York Philharmonic, Film Society of Lincoln Center, Chamber Music Society of Lincoln Center, Lincoln Center Theater, and Jazz at Lincoln Center – not to mention the Juilliard School and School of American Ballet – Lincoln Center offers something for every cultured appetite. Divine film series, swing dancing festivals, the Mostly Mozart concert, and Great Performers series are just the tip of the iceberg.

THEATERS

Ars Nova, 511 West 54th Street (10th Ave), Midtown West
Tel: 212 868 4444 www.arsnovanyc.com

A superbly run small black box theater where big-name performers put on small-batch shows and talented emerging acts get their first well-directed shots at excellence. With only 99 seats, it allows theater enthusiasts intimate access to acts like Sandra Bernhard, Liza Minelli, and Rufus Wainwright (at their most casual), while fun theater series and plenty of "next big things" take center stage.

Lucille Lortel, 121 Christopher Street (Bedford), West Village
Tel: 212 279 4200 www.lortel.org

Producing solely non-profit productions since the establishment of the Lucille Lortel Foundation in 1999, this handsome theater in the heart of the West Village is a great part of its community and offers satisfying productions from top directors, plus readings and benefits. The space, built in 1953, originally hosted productions of the Threepenny Opera, under the name Theatre de Lys – a gift from Lortel's industrialist husband, Louis Schweitzer.

New World Stages, 340 West 50th Street (6th Ave), Midtown West

Tel: 646 871 1730   www.newworldstages.com

Built in the former location of Madison Square Garden, the labyrinthine space offers comfortable seating throughout five subterranean theaters, with productions of several shows taking place consecutively. There are two bars, a lobby lounge and gallery, and auditorium spaces ranging in size from 199 seats to 499 seats.

Second Stage Theater, 307 West 43rd Street (8th Ave), Midtown West

Tel: 212 246 4422   www.2st.com

Nestled in the Theater District, this off-Broadway institution is known for its restagings of fine American plays that never took off at their debut (a.k.a. "second stagings"), and produces acclaimed off-Broadway debuts. Having launched big-name acts for nearly three decades, the company frequently welcomes its esteemed alum back to its stage.

MOVIE THEATERS

Angelika Film Center, 18 West Houston Street (Mercer), Noho

Tel: 212 995 2000   www.angelikafilmcenter.com

Despite the rumbling of the subway underneath, film buffs love this theater, with its open café, gourmet goodies upstairs, traditional movie junk food downstairs, and smashing selection of art-house movies.

Loews Lincoln Center & IMAX Theater, 1998 Broadway (W 68th St), Upper West Side

Tel: 212 336 5000

With 11 screens – including a dazzling, state-of-the-art IMAX arena – this is the premier spot for being blown away by the latest action flick.

Sunshine Cinema, 143 East Houston Street (Forsyth), Lower East Side
Tel: 212 330 8182 www.landmarktheatres.com

Hipsters flock to this great-looking theater with its cool décor, stadium seats, superb sound, gourmet food, and indie flicks – plus great film series.

Ziegfeld Theater, 141 West 54th Street (6th Ave), Midtown West
Tel: 212 765 7600

This glitzy, old-school movie palace was built in 1962, and has long been the site of film premieres and special film events. Its 306 balcony seats are a real treat, although any of its 1,100-plus seats feels special.

shop...

Oh, you lucky ducks! You've arrived in the Fashion Capital of the World! OK, maybe you're thinking, What about Paris, or London? Sure, Paris has the perennially chic thing going for it, and London is all about pushing fashion's boundaries – but there's all that and more to be found on this tiny island of Manhattan. Besides, there is no quantifying such a title, but for the sake of this book we'll assert – and many will agree – that New York is, in many ways, the Fashion Capital of the World.

It doesn't matter what your style or passion or fetish or weird collection is – New York has the kind of shopping you dream of. From department stores to designer boutiques, furniture emporiums to bespoke tailors, sporting Meccas to lingerie shops, vintage spots to sex stores, there's a marvelous way to flash your green. (In case you didn't realize, the money here is green). If you're a big, bad shopaholic, you may want to bring along a companion who's charged with keeping you in check, because dropping big dollars in this city is easier than you'd ever imagine possible.

For big spenders, there are several routes to take, though in all likelihood you'll wind up hitting Fifth and Madison Avenues in Midtown East and on the Upper East Side. There, you'll find all the big names flashing their finest wares, with

many designers operating their flagship stores there. You'll also probably visit the big gun department stores – Saks Fifth Avenue, Bloomingdale's, Neiman Marcus, Henri Bendel, Barneys New York. Don't forget Takashimaya, the gorgeous Japanese import that is a treat for all the senses.

For more downtown-oriented folks, there are plenty of treasures to be founds throughout Soho, plus all the chic eateries you'll need to keep your energy up. Do stroll through Prada's famous store designed by genius Rem Koolhass on Prince and Broadway before winding your way west on Prince Street and back east on Spring Street, making sure to explore Green Street, Wooster Street, and West Broadway. If you do feel inclined to do the whole knock-off Prada or Chanel bag search in Chinatown, that can be found on Canal Street – described by National Public Radio as the 'Kazaa of the fashion world', in reference to infamous website where copyrighted files were long-distributed for free. Nolita, Soho's little sister neighborhood lying to its east, is tremendously chic, and its smaller designers present shoppers with fresh ways to jazz up their wardrobes. Some Odd Rubies, Chip and Pepper, Ksubi, C. Ronson, and Tory Burch are just some of the necessary stopovers.

And then of course there's the West Village, the gorgeous, sleepy neighborhood that calls itself home to the famous, monied, and fashionable. Bleecker Street has become its main vein of chic shopping, with Marc Jacobs, Ralph Lauren, and Cynthia Rowley leading the pack. Near 14th Street the West Village turns into the Meatpacking District, which – in the last five years – has become to go-to spot for visionary designers like Alexander McQueen, Stella McCartney, Catherine Malandrino, and Diane von Furstenberg to roll out their awnings.

Happy, healthy spending, folks!

CHELSEA

WEST 18TH STREET

Barneys Co-Op (236) Offshoots of au courant department store Barneys New York, offering up-and-coming casualwear lines, marvelous beauty products, and superhip sneakers.
BoConcept (144) Many style and color variations available from this sleek Scandinavian design house that specializes in modular pieces.
Fisch For the Hip (158) The very best resale clothing for men and women, from suits to ready-to-wear to a well-edited selection of hard-to-get accessories.
West Elm (112) Approachable styles for bed, bath, and kitchen, with plenty of affordable ways to bring interior trends home.

ELSEWHERE

Balenciaga (542 West 22nd St) This far-West Chelsea boutique features the winning wares of Nicolas Ghesquiere, who has imbued the famed label with tough-girl sexiness and whimsy.
Comme Des Garçons (520 West 22nd St) Sought-after fashions from Japanese Rei Kawakubo, on display inside a space-age, pod-like boutique.
Jensen-Lewis (89 Seventh Avenue) Cavernous interiors stretching across an entire city block.
Karim Rashid (137 West 19th St) A wide array of colorful furniture, home gear, accessories, and fashion items from the award-winning designer.
Parke & Ronen (176 Ninth Avenue) Dapper selection of T-shirts, swimwear, smart trousers, and slim-fitting button-downs for men.
TSE (450 West 15th St) Ultra-luxurious cashmere for men, women, and baby, as well as heavenly ready-to-wear looks in stretch cotton twill.
202/Nicole Farhi (75 Ninth Avenue) Cool, classic looks for men and women, plus Farhi's high-end housewares, presented alongside her chic downtown café.

BOND STREET

Daryl K. (21) Precisely tailored, boundary-defying, sexy, and feminine, designer Daryl Kerrigan is the ultimate designer for edgy Downtown gals.
Ghost (28) Ethereal and timeless, the light-as-air creations of Tanya Sarne are beyond flattering and move with you.

BROADWAY

Adidas Sports Performance (610) A slick showroom for each of Adidas's lines of precision athletic footwear, just a hop, skip, and a jump from its sister store on Wooster Street where the label's casual styles reside.
American Apparel (712) One of many storefronts cropping up around town, the LA-based cotton purveyor pushes its perfect-fitting, multi-colored T-shirts, sweats, and throwback 1970s gym wear.
Atrium (644) Up-to-the-minute lines of premium denim and outerwear on a well-trafficked corner, appealing to adventurous dressers with cash to blow.
Urban Outfitters (628) Every hipster's go-to haven for right-this-minute trends, cool basics and sneakers, and well-chosen pieces from young-spirited lines like Diesel, Triple Five Soul, Evisu, and Le Tigre.

ELSEWHERE

Dave's Quality Meat (7 E 3rd St) Sneaker-philes always go back for seconds at this butcher-themed shop offering limited-edition lines of kicks and original Ts.
Jutta Neumann (158 Allen St) Hand-crafted leather goods with a hearty feel, from footwear to simple jewelry to clutches and shoulder bags.
Kiehl's (109 Third Avenue) The beloved apothecary, well stocked with everything your body wants in its various white bottles, plus generous samples and a knowledgeable staff.

Norman's Sound & Vision (67 Cooper Square) One of the city's most revered hard-to-find music outlets, with an impressive selection of jazz and plenty of bargain used CDs and DVDs.

NYC Velo (64 Second Avenue) True bike enthusiasts drool over the high-end selection, with the latest offerings from Javelin, Bianchi, and Ridley, plus cutting-edge gear.

Rafe (1 Bleecker St) Enviable handbags, shoes, and accessories by Rafe Totengo are fawned over by a tasteful clientele, who love to linger in the pretty environs of this Bowery boutique.

Rue St. Denis (170 Avenue B) One of the most meticulously managed vintage stores in town, with plenty of dapper, bygone looks for guys and shoes gals will flip for.

Some Odd Rubies (151 Ludlow St) A great mix of old and new pieces in a shoebox of a store, owned by a few chic gals including actress Summer Phoenix; key pieces have been resewn for more modern fits.

Trash and Vaudeville (4 St. Marks Place) A mainstay of the punk look (draining fast from this once hardcore neighborhood), specializing in bondage pants, rubber, and other garments your folks would have hated.

FINANCIAL DISTRICT/TRIBECA

Baker Tribeca (129–133 Hudson Street) Sizable furniture emporium in a former grain warehouse where Midwestern home company Baker Furniture displays its tasteful lines from the industry's top talent.

Century 21 (22 Cortlandt Street) The undeniable champ when it comes to designer clothing, beauty products, house wares, and shoes at bargain basement prices; wildly popular.

LuLuLemon Athletica (145 Chambers Street) Canadian athletic apparel company specializing in yoga garb for both sexes.

Thom Browne (100 Hudson Street) Cool purveyor of neat, perfectly cut men's suits reminiscent of the 1950s and '60s – including the signature high water trousers.

FLATIRON DISTRICT/UNION SQUARE

BROADWAY

ABC Carpet & Home (888) Six wonderful old floors of chic interior designs – from preppy antiques to worldly eclectic pieces to mid-century vintage offerings, plus an amazing selection of rugs on the top floor.

Bang & Olufsen (927) Sleek and futuristic, the esteemed stereo company boasts its best sound machines, speakers, and electronics.

Design Within Reach (903) An attractive, knowing staff walks a chic clientele through the mid-century's coolest offerings, and there's much more than Eames chairs.

Fish's Eddy (889) Designer lines of dishware are sold alongside unembellished plates and bowls, as well as vintage dishes from years gone by.

FIFTH AVENUE

Anthropologie (85) Feminine frocks and throwback homeware seemingly plucked from the country closet of some poet's muse.

Artistic Tile (79) More tile than you can shake a stick at – though we don't suggest shaking anything; these pre-mosaics are pricey.

Club Monaco (160) Wonderfully affordable wardrobe staples that go with nearly everything or quickly dress up an outfit in a pinch.

J. Crew (91) Great looking, approachable prepster fashions for men and women, colorfully presented on two airy floors.

Juicy Couture (103) Originally known for tedious velvet tracksuits that plagued Los Angeles, the hip brand has upped its originality and sexiness and opened a few very popular NYC outposts.

Paul Smith (108) Beautifully tailored and oh-so-dapper suits, colorful shirts, and accessories from a master British designer.

UNION SQUARE

American Eagle Outfitters (19) Everywhere you look, it's that cute college look – very Abercrombie, yet much friendlier on the wallet – plus there's a (slim) chance of finding something without an insignia on it.

Diesel (1) A slick, bi-level store, well stocked with the brand's famous jeans and plenty more trendsetting styles.

Adorama Camera (42 West 18th St) An all-you-need photo Mecca, where an experienced sales staff walks you through an unbeatable selection of used and new cameras, video equipment, darkroom gear, and lighting.

M.A.C. Cosmetics (1 East 22nd St) By makeup artists, for makeup artists, this vampy beauty line brings out the 1980s supermodel inside us all.

Trixie and Peanut (23 East 20th St) Hilarious displays hint at absolutely perfect doggie fashions, beds, accessories, and carriers inside.

Virgin Megastore (52 East 14th St) A perennially packed music and DVD emporium that seems to be holding up, even though everyone downloads their entertainment these days.

MEATPACKING DISTRICT

GANSEVOORT STREET

Buckler (13) You'll be all set to go from this subterranean men's store to a sold-out concert stage with Andrew Buckler's authentic rocker gear.

Theory (38) Kicked-up, ultra-flattering basics for men and women inhabit this recent outpost of the Theory brand.

Trina Turk (67) Sculptor and stylish dude Jonathan Adler designed the punchy environment that showcases designer Turk's throwback Americana pieces that fly off the shelves.

WEST 14TH STREET

Alexander McQueen (417) Britain's fashion renegade shows off his most wearable togs, shoes, and accessories for men and women in this sleek boutique that's worthy of the clothing's dramatic prices.

Bodum (413–15) The well-known purveyor of French press coffee makers shows off a full line of lovable appliances and dishware, in cool colors and stylish Euro designs.

DDC Lab (427) A sleek, slim storefront featuring future-forward designs, primo denim, and cool ready to wear gear.

Diane von Furstenberg (444) The ever-elegant queen of the emboldened female style (and creator of the wrap dress) offers delicious dresses and separates in picture-perfect prints.

Jeffrey New York (449) Stylish ladies and gents come to this runway-informed style emporium to worship; perusing the top name sunglasses, shoes, and ready-to-wear is a religious experience.

Stella McCartney (429) Don't come eating a hot dog to the boutique of high-end vegetarian designer McCartney, but do come ready to devour her lovely, perfectly flattering gear.

ELSEWHERE

An Earnest Cut & Sew (821 Washington St) The softest, subtlest scarves, cool-nerd button-downs and cardigans, and near-perfect jeans draw style hounds to this stylish, woody shop.

Ed Hardy (425 West 13th St) Clothes that won't soon be forgotten, outfitted with their unsubtle embellishments and tattoo artist emblems, are well stocked in this former warehouse that is equally unsubtle in its décor.

Scoop NYC (861 Washington St) A no-brainer for shoppers who need to look up-to-the-minute, regardless of cost – same goes for the nearby Scoop Men's and Scoop Kids.

Tracy Reese (641 Hudson St) Girly creations for grown-ups – shoes, bags, dresses, and separates – in a luscious pink setting.

MIDTOWN WEST/GARMENT DISTRICT/THEATER DISTRICT

Charles Tyrwhitt (745 Seventh Avenue) Dapper British menswear line, big on Sea Island shirts, ties that pop, and English welted leather shoes.

Manolo Blahnik (31 West 54th St) Making grown women drool, Blahniks rarely disappoint with their prime design, staggering heights, and sexy finishes.

Movado (610 Fifth Avenue) True precision tickers that add a little panache to any wrist; handsome, modern jewelry adds to the draw.

OMO Norma Kamali (11 West 56th St) Long-beloved fashion figure Kamali celebrates the female silhouette with her remarkable swimsuits, eveningwear, and suits.

Original Penguin (1077 Sixth Avenue) Cute-boy fashions from classic Munsingwear line on kitschy display.

The Sharper Image (50 Rockefeller Plaza) You may not need a talking potato peeler, but you want it – along with all of the Image's other slick guy gizmos.

Smythson of Bond Street (4 West 57th St) If this stationery is good enough for the Queen of England, it's good enough for you...

MURRAY HILL/MIDTOWN EAST

EAST 57TH STREET

Christian Dior (212) One of the most sought-after names in high fashion shows off in this deluxe storefront.

Jil Sander (11) Sexy simplicity is the rule of thumb for Sander's clientele, and the clothing – dramatic yet unembellished – screams luxury.

Louis Vuitton (1) Visit the lap of luxury at the flagship store of this legendary luxury company, presenting exquisite accessories, must-have handbags, and tempting togs for stylish guys and gals.

Niketown New York (6) More Nike sneakers and athletic gear than you ever imagined existed set in a hyperstimulating atmosphere.

Turnbull & Asser (42) Perhaps the most inviting high-end haberdashery in New York, this renowned British shirtmaker and suit purveyor is a businessman's dream store.

FIFTH AVENUE

Abercrombie & Fitch (721) The go-to spot for that all-American teen look, with a wide selection of jeans, logo-ed T-shirts, and slouch wear.

Bottega Veneta (699) The beautiful flagship store of the luxury Italian leather goods brand, where chic décor and peppy tunes implore shoppers to linger over its gorgeous bags, shoes, and accessories.

Cartier (653) Dazzling diamonds are just the tip of the "ice"-berg at this classic jeweler that is a standard-bearer of impeccable taste.

Ermenegildo Zegna (663) Deluxe suit purveyor, known for fab fabrics and fit made for the corner office.

Escada (715) For unrepentant glamour, big-spending gals get indulgent at this multi-level boutique featuring the revered brand's feminine accessories, separates, and haute couture.

FAO Schwartz (767) Travelers with kids can't get around a trip to this frenetic, fantastical toy emporium.

Gucci (685) Even without Tom Ford at the helm, this slinky, high-end clothier delivers jet-setter gear that makes everyone feel like a model.

Mikimoto (730) No pearls look fresher than these exquisite cultured beauties, decadently strung or set for a variety of tastes and situations.

Salvatore Ferragamo (655) For a 360-degree wardrobe that declares to the world opulence and taste, men and women turn to Italian fashion house Ferragamo; it never lets them down.

Tiffany & Co. (727) That little blue box sends heart aflutter, and a stroll through this classic jewelry shop will overstimulate shoppers with its glittering displays.

Versace (647) A lavish showcase for the sexy, spot-on wares of Donatella Versace, who has toned down the line a tad in recent years, yet never lost the panache.

MADISON AVENUE

Coach (595) Pretty bags, gloves, and accessories in sumptuous leathers, plus a delicious assortment of scarves conceived by talented designer Reed Krakoff.

Domenico Vacca (702) Super-expensive, supremely tailored Italian suits and button-downs as well as gorgeous Italian shoes draw a heavy-hitting set of shoppers.

Molton Brown (515) A British brand offering beautifully packaged skincare goods and cosmetics that don't scare off guys; great haircare products, too.

Paul Stuart (350) A well-suited gent's dream store, with respectful staffers, an unparalleled sock and tie selection, antique walking sticks, and an endless range of suit sizes and styles.

Brioni (55 East 52nd St) The very best in meticulous Italian suiting, plus a wholly capable staff that goes to great lengths to fit you. A second store up the way on 57th Street.

Chanel (3 West 57th St) This flagship displays all the must-have items, from handbags and ladylike suits to the classic perfumes.

NOLITA

ELIZABETH STREET

Hollywould (198) Boundary-pushing boots, kittenish heels, sumptuous sandals, and four-alarm flats from one of hipster New York's favorite cobblers.

Me & Ro (241) Delicate Indian- and Asian-inspired pieces – silver and 10-karat gold necklaces, dangly earrings, and darling rings.

Seize Sur Vingt (243) A dapper hipster's delight, this custom tailor and haberdashery offers shirts, suits, ties, and Italian shoes that run from quirky to luxurious.

Tory Burch (257) The queen of the haute tunic has the social and celeb scene in a trance, with her casual and more dressed-up pieces, alongside exceptional accessories.

MOTT STREET

Calypso (280) Designer Christiane Celle presents her breezy, bohemian garb – right out of the Hamptons or St. Moritz – alongside high-end labels that fit her vibe.

Mixona (262) The crème de la crème of lingerie lines the racks and adorns some of the sexiest mannequin displays in the city.

MULBERRY STREET

Cath Kidston (201) Originally a purveyor of adorable handbags, the line has expanded to include fabrics, housewares, and general lifestyle gear, all kicked up with enviable prints.

Chip & Pepper (250) The surfer vibe abounds in a hunting shack-themed storefront, with envy-inducing jeans, T-shirts, and surfer gear from a pair of blond twin brothers.

C. Ronson (239) Socialite-cum-designer Charlotte Ronson outfits her girlie T-shirts and undies with kitschy 1970s style and patterns she plumbed from her childhood sticker collection.

Malia Mills Swimwear (199) Mercifully, these smartly designed maillots suit a wide cross-section of body types, and look supersexy thanks to designer Mills's wizardry with fabric and shape.

Paul Frank (195) Clever Ts, undies, outerwear, and accessories for the kid in all of us – and for all our kids – in a bright, color-packed corner store.

SPRING STREET

Crumpler Bags (45) One of two downtown outposts that feature some of the most durable and daring messenger and camera bags out there; plenty of straps and cool colors from a great Down Under brand.

Fresh (57) Delicious beauty products in clean, straightforward packaging – from fragrance to make-up to candles and specialty lines of cleansers.

ELSEWHERE

Santa Maria Novella (285 Lafayette St) Delights for all senses abound at this Florentine beauty company, with its hoity-toity toiletries and gilded setting.

Sigerson Morrison (28 Prince St) Utterly addictive shoes that are big on sex appeal and color choice, set in a decidedly minimalist store.

SOHO

BROADWAY

Bloomingdale's Soho (504) The downtown outpost of the legendary department store, featuring younger lines and more progressive designers, plus a diving selection of shoes.

Prada (575) A stupefying space designed by Rem Koolhas – including a sloping floor and futuristic display areas – where Miuccia Prada's iconic duds get the star treatment.

The Scholastic Store (557) A wildly popular educational haven where little ones go crazy for their toys, not to mention the latest adventures of their favorite literary characters.

BROOME STREET

Alexis Bittar (465) Whimsical jewelry from a Brooklyn-born artist known for Lucite marvels, funky costume pieces, and sweet semiprecious baubles.

Kate Spade (454) Dainty, delicious handbags, shoes, housewares, and accessories for the gal who longs for a simpler time.

Nanette Lepore (423) Eclectic throwback looks for the discerning, ladylike shopper, set in a pink-and-white birdcage-themed spot with a killer staircase.

GREENE STREET

Anna Sui (113) Irresistible 1960s-style parlor where Sui's vampy bohemian creations are on grand display.

Cloak (10) A clubby throwback showroom displaying slim suits and dark, Eastern European model gear that brings out the vampire in any guy.

Diesel Denim Gallery (68) Super-specific, limited edition jeans, presented like precious works of art, from one of the most trusted names in denim.

Jack Spade (56) Timeless totes, briefcases, and accessories presented in a cool, otherworldly atmosphere.

Jill Stuart (100) The celebrated designer presents seasonal celebrations of guiltless girly style, complete with plenty of frills and trendsetting touches.

La Perla (93) Outrageously sexy undies at eye-popping prices, from hose and garters to bustiers and beyond.

Montblanc (120) An intimate setting in which to peruse some of the finest writing implements in the world.

Moss (146 & 150) Marvelously conceived space where modern high-end furnishings are on brilliant display.

Nicole Miller (77) Approachable glamour is Miller's M.O., be it her slinky eveningwear or cool-gal separates.

LAYFAYETTE STREET

G-Star Raw (270) Super durable denim and highly styled hipster gear spread out over two floors on the Nolita/Soho precipice.

Triple Five Soul (290) Well-made, boundary-pushing gear that runs the gamut from "urban skateboarder" to "hip-hop star" to "computer genius."

MERCER STREET

Agent Provocateur (133) Chic outlet for kitten-with-a-whip lingerie, satin-tie corsets, throwback pantyhose, and transformative bustiers, as well as perfumes and high-end naughty things.

A.P.C. (131) Luxury French denim and tees that fit like a dream; perfect for scoring a few pieces that will go with everything.

Marni (161) "Boho chic" never looked better than on the racks at this dreamlike boutique, with its smock-like dresses and modish Italian accessories.

UGG Australia (79) More than just the über-comfy lined boots that have taken the world by storm; plenty of sandals, accessories, and outerwear, too.

PRINCE STREET

Apple Store (103) Offering the latest Mac products, services, and tutorials; perennially packed yet so sleek that you won't mind much.

Calvin Klein Underwear (104) The master of unmentionables shows off form-fitting skivvies around the corner from the infamous billboard that made them famous.

FACE Stockholm (110) Swedish makeup mavens bring bold colors and long-lasting essentials to a bustling Soho corner.

Intermix (98) The one-stop shop for the trendiest, most form-fitting offerings of the moment, from designers both up-and-coming and tried-and-true.

SPRING STREET

Burberry (131) A slick downtown store for Britain's most notorious purveyor of plaid; pricey essentials and top-notch trenches.
J. Lindeberg Stockholm (126) Boundary-pushing rock-star gear for everyday living, plus a special golf line for looking loose on the links.
John Varvatos (122) A well-manned storefront for this pioneer of understated, classic American menswear.
MoMA Design Store (81) Cutting-edge furniture, design books, dreamlike gadgetry, and one-of-a-kind jewelry in an exceptionally designed space by pioneering architect Richard Gluckman.

THOMPSON STREET

L'Artisan Parfumeur (68) Distinctive scents from the celebrated French perfume purveyors, set in a girlish jewel box.

WEST BROADWAY

DKNY (420) Donna Karan's reasonably priced urbanwear that takes its cues from New York street style.
Miss Sixty (386) Youthful, form-hugging jeans and saucy separates make this a favorite among women with bodies of sin.

WOOSTER STREET

Costume National (108) Sleek, timeless wardrobe essentials reminding us that black is always the new black.
Desiron (151) A sprawling showroom for the minimalist chic of this luxury Italian home line.
Todd Oldham for La-Z-Boy (73) The former fashion designer and king of eclectic chic takes on everyone's favorite recliner, to smashing results.

MADISON AVENUE

Akris (835) A cool, old-school setting for the line's flagship boutique, where style-savvy shoppers swoon for the exquisitely conceived dresses and separates.

Barbour by Peter Elliot (104) Gentlemanly clothing from a classic British brand that conjures up scene of weekend hunting retreats in the country – in a store to match.

Calvin Klein (654) The classically cool, all American design house offers casualwear and evening looks that are often black, plus simple, modern homewares.

Carolina Herrera (954) Arguably the most elegant American designer; these exquisite womenswear looks never go out of style.

Cesare Paciotti (833) If the shoe fits, you're lucky, since the Paciotti brand delivers exquisite ladies' footwear alongside the classically cool men's shoes that started the company half a century ago.

Chopard (725) Dazzling watches, jewelry, and accessories in candy colors, plus china, scarves, pens, and more.

Donna Karan (819) The first lady of fashion shows off chic urban ready-to-wear and night-time looks, not to mention exquisite shoes, in a serene, Asian-inspired setting.

Fred Leighton Rare Collectibles (773) Marvelous antique jewelry – including plenty of wonderful wedding rings and estate pieces – are drooled over by discerning customers who know that bling, like wine, gets better with age.

Frette (799) Dreamy sheets with superhigh thread counts that are a favorite of four-star hotels and celebrities the world over.

Giorgio Armani (760) A multi-floored oasis, where the Armani aesthetic immerses customers as they salivate over beautifully made, trend-defying clothing and shoes that look amazing on anyone.

Giuseppe Zanotti Design (806) Hard-to-resist heels, boots, and sandals from a master Italian shoe designer; they trade on sex appeal and don't come cheap.

Hermes (691) So much more than scarves your mother would love; exquisite bags (need we mention the Birkin or the Kelly), home goods, accessories, and ready-to-wear.

Issey Miyake (802) You'll get an eyeful poring over the innovative Japanese designs that are at times pretty, at times out-there, and at times pretty out-there.

Jo Malone (946) Elegantly presented beauty products and fragrances from a big name in the British beauty biz.

Loro Piana (821) The finest fabrics, including decadent cashmere for men and women, alongside classic, grown-up separates.

Michael Kors (974) Billed as the champion of classic American style, Kors offers beyond-chic casual wear, perfect for yachting, lounging, or cocktailing.

Miu Miu (831) The fun-loving ready-to-wear line from Miuccia Prada, complete with smashingly cute shoes and well-tailored separates.

Oliver Peoples (755) The new go-to sunglass brand of the boldfaced set, with sizes big, sleek, or subtle that suit even hard-to-flatter faces.

Sonia Rykiel (849) Slender and beautifully crafted, Rykiel's delicate suits, separates, and knit sweaters are much loved.

Tod's (650) Driving moccasins aren't necessary in the city, but they certainly are nice to have when they are Tod's, as are the luxe leather accessories.

Wolford (996) Hosiery goes super high end, with plenty of expensive, perfectly made, stretchy, sheer offerings and bodysuits.

ELSEWHERE

Asprey (50 East 57th St) Marvelous, classic British label, offering enviable silver, top-notch timepieces, as well as more decadent versions that take their cues from the royal jewels.

Bulgari (3 West 5th St) Exquisite jewelry and watch collections that never fail to make a statement with its healthy helping of diamonds, gemstones, and 18 karat gold.

Dylan's Candy Bar (1011 Third Avenue) Kids go absolutely insane for this Wonka-like sugar shack from Ralph Lauren's daughter, Dylan... Chances are you'll find something that delights you, too.

Kate's Paperie (140 West 57th St) A vast, beautiful selection of stationery, wrapping, cards, rubber stamps, organizers, and writing implements.

Nicole Farhi (10 East 60th St) London fashion fave Farhi artfully displays her men's and women's wear as well as home goods, while feeding well-heeled customers at her popular restaurant Nicole's.

UPPER WEST SIDE

Beau Brummel (287 Columbus Avenue) If you're not afraid to show your inner dandy, this dapper men's store should suit your needs nicely.

Betsey Johnson (248 Columbus Avenue) For fruity, frisky looks that span the aesthetic gambit from Hamptons cocktail party to East Village punk bar, Johnson's boutique is the one-stop shop.

Toga Bikes (110 West End Avenue) A wonderland for leisure bikers as well as pros, this bike emporium has the latest and greatest for cyclists.

WEST VILLAGE

BLEECKER STREET

Bond No. 9 (399) Perfume lines devoted to different Manhattan neighborhoods – and a service that will mix them up to your liking – on a ritzy Bleecker Street block.

Cynthia Rowley (376) Humor interjects itself into Rowley's sexy styles, making every gal feel adorable; they're on fine display at this sweet throwback store.

James Perse (361) Cool Californian Perse offers unbeatably soft T's, dresses, and pants for ladies who like to keep it simple; a men's store is just a quick stroll down Bleecker.

Lulu Guinness (394) Irresistible, adorable handbags for any occasion, sold alongside cutie-pie accessories in a boutique that's all open arms.

L'Uomo (383) A handsome, luxury-laden spot where a well-edited selection of men's suits, dress shirts and casualwear lures dudes of distinction.

Marc by Marc Jacobs (403–5) Fashion darling Jacobs at his most accessible and playful, in adjoining men's and women's boutiques – plus a separate accessories store down the block.

Olive & Bette's (384) A flirtatious selection of clean-lined, pure Americana ready-to-wear, as well as cutesy jewelry and accessories.

Polo Ralph Lauren (380) The grand poobah of preppy panache at his most laid-back best, with plenty of weekending and sports gear.

Selima Optique (357) Sensational specs in an array of colors and styles – 100 shapes in all – that flatter any face, and will cost you.

GREENWICH AVENUE

Flight 001 (96) Sleek and quirky travel gear – including luggage, special themed survival kits, wallets and luggage tags, and laptop totes – in an upbeat environment.

Mxyplyzyk (125) You never know what luxurious non-essential item you'll stumble upon at this adorable shop named for a comic book villain.

ELSEWHERE

The Bathroom (94 Charles St) A gorgeous shop to peruse through an unbeatable selection of top and hard-to-find beauty brands and home products.

Catherine Malandrino (652 Hudson St) The flagship store of the French design star, where a dazzling, store-length chandelier and slick furniture strike a dramatic stage for Malandrino's textural, feminine creations.

Christian Louboutin (59 Horatio St) Strut like a true Parisian in these red-soled stunners that cost as much as your arm and leave a trail of envy in your wake.

Hable Construction (117 Perry St) The most adorable prints grace everything from pillows to aprons to picture frames, while ornaments, embroidered quilts, and oven mitts turn houses to homes.

DEPARTMENT STORES

Barneys New York, 660 Madison Avenue (E 61st St), Upper East Side

Tel: 212 826 8900 www.barneys.com

Open: 10am–8pm Mon–Fri; 10am–7pm Sat; 11am–6pm Sun

There are several great department stores in New York, but none get fashionable hearts so a-flutter as this gorgeous fashion mecca that draws stylephiles from all over. Customers know that if it's au courant, Barneys will have it, be it the company's eponymous luxury line; soft offerings from emerging lines such as Loomstate; enduring elegance from Diane von Furstenberg; drop-dead-gorgeous denim from Acne Jeans; Ksubi, or Levi's

Capital E; or strut-worthy shoes from Giuseppe Zanotti, Martin Margiela, Lanvin, or Ann Demeulemester. Men are hardly left out, with its cool selection of sportswear and guy-friendly grooming products. Cosmetics and skin-care, meanwhile, are nothing but the best – new products from Natura Bisse, NARS, Chantecaille, and Aesop. Don't leave without taking a little turn through the home goods, tableware, and stationery. Barneys boasts three Co-op stores – one in Soho, another in Chelsea, and another in the West 70s – where the youngest looks get their day to shine.

Bergdorf Goodman, 754 Fifth Avenue (57th), Midtown East
Tel: 212 753 7300 www.bergdorfgoodman.com
Open: 10am–8pm Mon–Fri; 10am–7pm Sat; noon–6pm Sun

A long-revered mainstay of chichi styles, Bergdorf's draws in the jet set and lunching ladies with its mind-blowing selection of artfully arranged shoes, accessories, cosmetics, and clothes. Younger style setters go crazy over the haute denim, and more contemporary lines like Elie Tahari, M Missoni, Tory Burch, and Rebecca Taylor. Grand dames, meanwhile, can pore over the very latest YSL, Armani, and Oscar de la Renta. Visionary designers such as Proenza Schouler, Gaultier, Chloé, and Zac Posen are right at home. The beauty section rivals any other in existence, and the jewelry and accessories come from names like Stephen Dweck, Tom Ford Eyewear, Leiber, and Paul Morelli. The men's store, Bergdorf Goodman Men's, is located just a quick stroll away at 745 Fifth Avenue, offering both contemporary and traditional looks, plus a fantastic selection of shoes. Think: Zegna, Dsquared2, Burberry, Rock & Republic, and AG Adriano Goldschmied.

Bloomingdale's, 1000 Third Avenue (E 59th St), Upper East Side
Tel: 212 705 2000 www.bloomingdales.com
Open: 10am–8pm Mon–Fri; 11am–7pm Sat/Sun(daily, 9am–10pm December)

Beloved for its vast selection, Art Deco beauty, and status as a go-to desti-nation for looks both affordable and aspirational, this block-sized depart-ment store has drawn in spend-happy crowds since the late 1800s, offering an extensive selection of men's, women's, and children's wear, plus bedding collections from top designers, fine kitchen gear, and houseware. On the clothes front, women will find everything from Michael Kors to Juicy Couture, plus high-end denim like Rich & Skinny and True Religion. Men find Lacoste, Calvin Klein, Andrew Marc, and BOSS Hugo Boss. Don't forget to peruse the extensive shoe section, where Nanette Lepore flats commingle with Lilly Pulitzer espadrilles and futuristic wedges from Stuart Weitzman.

Henri Bendel, 712 Fifth Avenue (56th St), Midtown East
Tel: 212 247 1100 www.henribendel.com
Open: 10am–8pm Mon–Sat; noon–7pm Sun

One of the most transporting shopping experiences in town, this four-floor department store – graced by exquisite Lalique windows and a striking spiral staircase – is a glorious mish-mash of divine, youth-driven styles, right below Central Park. Hard-to-track-down designers and giants of the garment trade splay their latest wares for Upper East Side beauties and downtown sophisticates alike, while up-to-the-minute cosmetics and skincare are meticulously selected and reverentially displayed. If a little lingerie is in order, you can't do better than the skivvies on floor three. Although it's owned by Limited Brands (owners of Victoria's Secret and Express), Bendels retains a sense of mom-and-pop charm.

Macy's, 151 West 34th Street (Broadway), Midtown
Tel: 212 695 4400 www.macys.com
Open: 10am–9pm Mon–Sat; 11am–8pm Sun

A city landmark, Macy's – one entire bustling block of consumer-driven glee – moved to its present location in 1902, installing the grand wooden escalators that are still in use today. Aside from boasting an enormous stock of approachable merchandise over seven floors, Macy's is truly a part of the city's culture, producing the annual Thanksgiving parade and the city's fireworks show on the Fourth of July. It was also the first store to introduce an in-store Santa Claus at Christmas time. History aside, Macy's offers a huge selection for men, women, kids, and the home, plus an increasing presence of higher-end designer wares. Yes, tourists come in droves – but so do everyday New Yorkers, because it always warrants a visit, no matter who you are.

Saks Fifth Avenue, 611 Fifth Avenue (50th St), Midtown
Tel: 212 753 4000 www.s5a.com
Open: 10am–8pm Mon–Fri, 10am–7pm Sat; noon–7pm Sun

Get tempted by the coolest department store website ever, s5a.com, then
head in to this gorgeous, 10-floor Mecca for glamorphiles. Nearly every mid-
priced and high-end designer line you could hope to find is on hand, spanning the categories of shoes, beauty, handbags, jewelry, swim, accessories,
children's, men's, and of course, women's apparel. While the Saks brand has
reached far and wide throughout the country and world, this is the store
that started it all, and arguably refined what a high-end department store is
supposed to feel like. Plenty of themed events and sales make every visit
unique. If you've got the bucks to spend, splurge on the Fifth Avenue Club,
Saks's knowledgeable personal shopping service.

Takashimaya, 693 Fifth Avenue (54th St), Midtown East
Tel: 212 350 0100
Open: 10am–7pm Mon–Sat; noon–5pm Sun

This absolutely gorgeous Japanese department store (the only US outpost)
puts a spin on the idea of one-stop shopping, with its marvelous, artistic displays, serene décor, cosseting staff, and gorgeous offerings in everything from
home décor to apparel to electronics. The beauty floor is the stuff of leg-
ends, featuring products not normally available stateside. Vintage furnishings
will surprise even hardened interiors snobs. The tea salon is a rejuvenating
spot, with its vast selection of teas and light, elegant fare. The florist on the
main floor creates wildly popular arrangements, a favorite of fashion companies looking to impress clients and editors.

Time Warner Center, 10 Columbus Circle (59th St), Midtown West
Tel: 212 484 8000 www.shopsatcolumbuscircle.com

The latest New York landmark is a magnificent sight to behold, housing
everything a visitor could want, including an enormous Whole Foods market, the Mandarin Oriental hotel, magnificent restaurants, and the spectacular Jazz at Lincoln Center space, where aficionados can hear the genre's top
performers in three spaces, sometimes while overlooking Central Park.

Originally the AOL – Time Warner Center (before the companies parted ways), these futuristic towers have been enthusiastically embraced by the city, and strolling shoppers have plenty to take in. Here are some of its top offerings:

The Art of Shaving Shop Perfectly presented products for the gentlemen among us

A/X Armani Exchange Armani's most affordable, approachable line

Bebe Popular, flirtatious looks that bold women love to wear and men love to ogle

Bose The first name in precision sound systems

Godiva Chocolatier The world's most popular high-end chocolate purveyor

Montmartre A top notch collection of flirty, feminine ready to wear clothes, accessories, and shoes

Morgenthal Frederics Sensational specs in plenty of fashion colors and styles

Sephora Smell, look, and feel gorgeous with this wildly popular beauty emporium

Williams-Sonoma The home goods and kitchenware mainstay.

Shopping List

play...

If you come to New York and find yourself bored, you aren't doing it right. Get out there and push your boundaries! Did you really come here to watch primetime television in your hotel rooms? Unlikely, people. Now, it was laughably impossible to include everything about New York in this little black book. (That was the point, actually... Not everything, just our favorites.) But do with the city what you will – the more you push, the more you'll find. In this section, you'll find some delightful and fascinating ways to enjoy New York that don't involve stuffing yourself, imbibing wildly or maxing out your credit cards.

If your body is your temple, use it in wildly inventive ways. Rent a bike and hit the Hudson River Park and Riverside Park on the west side of the city, where you'll pedal alongside the city's fittest constituents as the Hudson River keeps you inspired (Even New Jersey looks beautiful from a distance!). Or better yet, take it in and around Central Park, where the masses come to decompress and check each other out. Here – and in Brooklyn's Prospect Park – you'll find every sport being enjoyed, including ice-skating, Frisbee, and our favorite, roller-dancing. There are many other parks for your cavorting pleasure, too – each a nerve center of its home neighborhood; each a place built to remind people who live in little boxes what it's like to watch the grass grow.

All this intensity can, of course, make things a tad stressful at times. If that happens, and you really are all about indulging yourself, then check out our hot list of worthy spas and their delish menus of treatments. The Mandarin Oriental hotel's services will transport you to the outer stratosphere, while

the kitschy, luxuriant treatment at Bliss lives up to its name. The Great Jones Spa in Noho will massage you, remove your hair, and supe up your skin, Feng Shui-style – they'll even provide you a 'cleansing' experience that will shrink-wrap you, in case you've got a big event to attend with lots of flashbulbs.

The city is not all sky-scrapers, neon, and hustle and bustle… and it will bend over backwards to please you if you let it. When the weather per-mits, there are live per-formances in most parks, or you can simply lay in the grass and watch the wonderful weirdos stroll by. In NYU student-saturated Washington Square Park, acoustic guitars and impromp-tu sing-alongs are commonplace. In Union Square, the skateboarders try new tricks as chic diners look on from the sidewalk seating of Coffee Shop or Republic on Union Square West. Central Park offers a million pleasant pastimes, while a visit to Prospect Park in Brooklyn will find sports ranging from cricket to kite-flying to Frisbee.

If you don't really know where to start your exploring, pick a tour that suits your style and let an expert orient you in style. If you're in the market for a break from this onslaught of humanity (or are an untamed animal inside), drop in on one of the city's very worthy zoos. And if none of this sound appealing, just grab a newspaper and a park bench… The rest will work itself out. Enjoy!

CYCLING

Bicycle Habitat, 244 Lafayette Street (Spring), Soho
Tel: 212 431 3315 www.bicyclehabitat.com
Open: daily, 10am–7pm (6.30pm Fri, 6pm Sat/Sun)

A fun, well-staffed bike emporium that not only sells the hottest street and mountain bikes – alongside the gear you need – but rents out an assortment of bikes for a flat fee of $50 per day.

Chelsea Bicycles, 156 West 26th Street (7th Ave), Chelsea
Tel: 212 727 7278 www.chelseabicycles.net
Open: 10am–8pm Mon–Sat; 11am–7pm Sun

At this Westside wheelie haven, you can grab yourself custom rides or wheels, or borrow a basic hybrid for $6 per hour, $35 per day. There's a discount for weekly rentals. High-end road bikes – the type Lance Armstrong would ride – will run you between $17.50 and $25 per hour.

Gotham Bike Shop, 112 West Broadway (Reade), Financial District
Tel: 212 732 2453 www.togabikes.com
Open: 10am (10.30am Sun)–6.30pm (7.30pm Thurs, 5pm Sun)

With a vast array of biking gear for the novice and the pro, this downtown shop is perfect for renting, then zipping up the piers along the west side of the city. Hybrid bikes go for $30 per day and $150 per week.

Toga Bike Shop, 110 West End Avenue (W 64th St), Upper West Side
Tel: 212 799 9625 www.togabikes.com
Open: 11pm (10am Sat)–7pm (8pm Thurs, 6pm Sat/Sun)

Touting itself as the city's oldest and largest bike retailer, Toga services the Upper West Side with a full range of bikes and gear, plus rentals that will run you $35 per day for a cruiser. If you are after a higher-end road bike, call ahead to check availability.

HELICOPTER FLIGHTS

Liberty Helicopters, West 30th St (12th Ave), West Chelsea
Tel: 212 967 6464   www.libertyhelicopters.com

Take a tour up and down the Hudson either during the day or as the sun-sets over Manhattan, although flights are, understandably, not allowed over the island itself. The Big Apple Tour weighs in at $119 per person and takes 12 minutes, but you get to fly around Lady Liberty and back up towards Central Park, giving passengers a fantastic visual picture of the city.

ICE-SKATING

Kate Wollman Rink, Prospect Park, Brooklyn
Tel: 718 287 6431   www.prospectpark.org

This marvelous skate park is a real treat – uncrowded and set against the verdant backdrop of Brooklyn's most glorious park.

Riverbank State Park, 679 Riverside Drive, Harlem
Tel: 212 694 3600

Set alongside the West Side Highway and high above the Hudson River, this canopied rink – plus a host of other sporting fields and courts – is located inside the city's only state park (something locals don't often realize).

Wollman Rink, Fifth Avenue (65th St), Upper East Side
Tel: 212 439 6900   www.wollmanskatingrink.com

The big cheese of city skating rinks (well, perhaps it shares the title with Rockefeller Center), Wollman Rink is operated these days by the Trump organization, so you know it's well maintained.

PARKS

Battery Park City, Battery Place (State), Financial District
Tel: 212 344 3491 www.batteryparkcity.org

Offering dramatic riverside views, gardens, playgrounds, and plazas, these 36 acres of open space at Manhattan's southernmost tip are a vital, iconic part of the city's culture. A wide variety of warm-weather programs and events includes everything from family days to "drawing in the park" programs to rock concerts, while many prefer to simply spread out on the lawn of Wagner Park and take in the sun and choice view of the Statue of Liberty. The Esplanade is prime people-watching territory, and World Financial Center (WFC) Plaza offers access to restaurants and plenty of nearby spots where you can grab a bite.

Bryant Park, 40th St (5th Ave), Midtown West
Tel: 212 768 4242 www.bryantpark.org

Between the wireless internet access throughout the park, the plentiful green folding chairs that call thousands of lunching business folk and tourists alike, and the hugely popular summertime movie and concert series, Bryant Park pulls out all the stops to make the public feel at home. Located behind the New York Public Library, these eight acres of lawn are utterly civilized, boasting an ornate French carousel, chess tables, food kiosks (including one from Tom Colicchio's marvelous Wichcraft; see Snack), and decidedly down-tempo air in comparison to the frenetic pace of Midtown that encircles it. The space boasts a multi-century history – it was traversed by Revolutionary soldiers, and was a potting field in the mid-1800s – and has been called Bryant Park since 1884, when it was renamed (from Reservoir Square) in honor of poet and newspaper editor William Cullen Bryant. While the Great Depression turned it decidedly seedy, the controversial, revolutionary city planner and parks commissioner Robert Moses used his muscle to bring it some of the spectacle visitors see today.

Central Park, 59th St to 110th St (5th Ave), Midtown West
Tel: 212 360 3444 www.centralpark.com

New York City's greatest treasure, Central Park is an expansive green space, 150 years old, that covers 843 acres and offers outdoor enthusiasts pretty much anything their hearts could desire against the dramatic backdrop of the city's architecture. Designed as a refuge for the cramped city in 1858 by Frederick Law Olmstead and Calvert Vaux, Central Park (lovingly maintained by the Central Park Conservancy) holds a special place in the heart of every New Yorker, from its horse-drawn carriages to its 136 acres of woodlands and the scenic views from the shores of its lake. Perpetually encircled by runners, cyclists, and rollerbladers, the park hosts big-draw events with its Center Park Summerstage series, Shakespeare in the Park, productions by the Metropolitan Opera and New York Philharmonic, and occasionally megaconcerts, like the one famously given by Simon and Garfunkel in 1981 that drew a crowd of 500,000. That is all just the tip of the iceberg. Beyond that, you can enjoy world-famous fountains (such as the iconic "Bethesda" at the lake and the Egyptian obelisk "Cleopatra's Needle"), placid gardens, ice-skating, the zoo, dinner at Tavern on the Green, the breathtaking reservoir, walking or biking tours, chilling out by the rollerskating dancers at the Skate Circle (endlessly entertaining), or simply tossing a Frisbee and catching some rays on any of the park's fantastic lawns (including the Great Lawn, Strawberry Fields, and Sheep's Meadow).

Hudson River Park, Battery Place to West 59th Street at the West Side Highway, Upper West Side
Tel: 212 627 2020   www.hudsonriverpark.org

This bustling stretch of bike and pedestrian paths, dotted with public and private piers, has come a long way in recent years, metamorphosing from what was a seedy, dangerous waterfront into a series of children's parks, sporting fields, dog runs, and much more. Most famous are the Christopher Street Piers, which remain to this day a super-social gathering place for sun worshipers – many of them gay men – who lie out, grab food, and socialize here as soon as the weather gets nice. City athletes perpetually run, roll, and bike up and down its serene pathways, urged on by the hum of the West Side Highway and the colorful crowds beside them. There are plenty of institutions that line the 550-acre park, including the Frying Pan nightclub at Pier 63, Chelsea Piers, and Riverside Park.

Madison Square Park, Madison Avenue (23rd St), Flatiron
Tel: 212 538 6667   www.madisonsquarepark.org

A much-needed public green space in the Flatiron District (since nearby Gramercy Park is fenced in), this 6.2 acre park is the go-to spot for local businesspeople and travelers who indulge in its recently introduced free wireless internet, abundant benches, green lawns, experimental sculpture, and outrageously popular snack stand from restaurateur Danny Meyer, the Shake Shack (see Snack; but be aware that the lines for this haute food kiosk get incredibly long, so if you're hungry line up early or bring a bag lunch). The site of the first baseball club, formed by Alexander Cartwright in 1845, as well as the location of P.T. Barnum's original circus performances, the Park has a long, varied history: two former Madison Square Gardens lined it; the arm and torch of the Statue of Liberty were displayed here as funds were raised to complete the structure; America's first community Christmas tree was illuminated here in 1912, and so on. The Madison Square Park Conservancy renovated the park in the 1990s, when it was badly in need of some TLC, and continues to raise funds for its maintenance.

Riverside Park, 72nd Street to 158th Street at the Hudson River, Upper West Side
Tel: 212 870 3070

A bike-lover's dream, this picturesque, four-mile-long waterfront park on Manhattan's Upper West Side/Harlem border – designed by Central Park and Prospect Park co-designer Frederick Law Olmstead – offers transporting views of the Hudson River and features a charming public marina plus public basketball, volleyball, and tennis courts. It is also the site of Grant's Tomb and the Warsaw Ghetto Uprising Monument. Be careful crossing into the park, since cars tend to zip through as they come off the nearby highway. Once inside, however, let your cares disappear as you wander, linger, or play. If you have energy to burn, follow the park south and meet up with the Hudson River Park, which takes you along the piers down to southern Manhattan.

Union Square Park, 14th St (Broadway), Flatiron
Tel: 212 460 1208

Located at the apex of the Flatiron District, Chelsea, the East Village, and the West Village, Union Square Park is one of the most vibrant public spaces in the city. It draws crowds young and old to sit on its 14th Street-facing steps, lounge on its grass, take in its fantastic Farmers' Market (Mondays, Wednesdays, and Saturdays), enjoy its holiday-time craft fair, and mix and mingle while going about their day. With free music and entertainment series in the summer, prime shopping and dining along its periphery, a children's park, a dog park, the very Sex & the City-esque seasonal restaurant Luna Park, and much more (plus one of the city's most active subway systems underneath it all) it is a prime cultural hub.

Washington Square Park, Waverly Place and 4th St, between University and MacDougal, Greenwich Village

The cultural heart of Downtown bohemian culture and nerve-center of New York University, this 9.75-acre space is recognizable by Washington's Arch (at the base of Fifth Avenue) and its famous fountain at the center, where performers entertain mass crowds on sunny weekends. Around the park you'll find all types: NYU classes taking al fresco sessions, novice musicians jamming, families young and old playing on the grass, locals letting their dogs loose in the flirty dog park, and vibrant characters from every corner of the city reading, laughing, and checking each other out. Its history is long and varied; before the city society depicted in Edith Wharton's books called the park and its surrounding area home, it was Native American marshland that was then claimed by the Dutch. Interestingly (don't let this dissuade you, now), there are approximately 20,000 bodies buried beneath the park, due to its former status as a "potter's field" during the yellow fever epidemics of the late-1700s. It was also the backdrop for the terrible Triangle Shirtwaist Company Fire, where 146 workers died as a result of unsafe working conditions. Onto happier times (sort of), Washington Square was the heart of beatnik and folk culture in the 1940s, '50s, and '60s, and to this day retains some of its renegade artistic air (although a severe clampdown on the drug dealers and seedy types of yore has stolen some of that rough-hewn charm). Today, it hosts a daily mix of diverse locals – from families to wackos – and you'll be glad you were a part of it.

SPAS

Amore Pacific, 114 Spring Street (Mercer), Soho
Tel: 212 966 0400   www.amorepacific.com
Open: daily, 11am (noon Sun)–7pm (8pm Thurs)

A divine day spa from a top Asian skincare line (known for their exquisite eye cream), this elegant spa offers green tea therapies, "five element" botanical healing facials, sculpting masques for the body and face, waxing, and more. Estheticians consult with each customer and craft a spectacular program for them using the renowned products that are the cornerstone of the brand and adhering to the philosophy that "true beauty emanates from within."

Bliss Soho, 2nd floor, 568 Broadway (Prince), Soho
Tel: 212 219 8970 www.blissworld.com
Open: 9am–9pm Mon–Fri; 9.30am–6.30pm Sat; 10am–6pm Sun

This super-popular beauty haven offers more than just delicious products; at this flagship spa locale, weary travelers feel their cares melt into luxury and rejuvenate in time to take the city by storm. Top estheticians, massage therapists, and manicurists offer adorably named services that feel great and work like a charm. Don't miss the "Herbie" (fruit acid wash and facial), the ginger rub (135 massage), reflexology, or the anti-cellulite "Quadruple Thighpass," then make sure you score a Spa-at-Home kit.

Cornelia Day Resort, 8th floor, 663 Fifth Avenue (W 53rd St), Midtown West
Tel: 212 871 3050 www.cornelia.com
Open: 9am–9pm Mon–Fri; 9am–7pm Sat; 11am–6pm Sun

This cosseting, full service spa – spread over two levels in an easy-to-miss office building in Midtown – is where worn-out celebrities and big shots go to be restored to their glorious, glowing selves. The elegantly appointed rooms and signature scent of citrus and sandalwood please the senses right off the bat, while relaxation rooms allow the mind to rest before and after the services. From nails, body masks, futuristic facials, and waxing to prenatal massage and lymphatic drainage, Cornelia hits its marks and does things right.

Exhale, 980 Madison Avenue (E 76th St), Upper East Side
Tel: 212 561 6400 www.exhalespa.com
Open: 7.30am–9pm Mon–Fri; 8am–8pm Sat/Sun

The Eastern-influenced luxuries of this 10,000-square-foot top-notch spa (and its sister location on Central Park South) offer personal training instruction, yoga classes, and expert massage and beauty services, not to mention transporting environments courtesy of interior designer Jason Lamberth. Acupuncture and nutritionist services are on hand, as are mind-blowing deep-tissue massages and gentleman's facials.

Townhouse Spa, 39 West 56th Street (5th), Midtown West

Tel: 212 245 8006 www.townhousespa.com

Open: daily, 10am–8pm

Billing itself as a "lavish social spa," the Townhouse invites its guests to take their time post-treatment, with ultra-luxurious relaxation rooms on separate men's and women's floors. All the trappings of a true deluxe spa are here – facials, steam rooms, waxing, and various massages – plus the private Phoenix Suite, where a guest can unwind in solitude in front of an LDC screen TV and dip into their own private steam and shower.

SPORTS CENTERS

Chelsea Piers, West Side Highway (24th St), Chelsea

Tel: 212 336 6666 www.chelseapiers.com

The city's premier sports center, this unmissable, 28-acre complex along the Hudson River has pretty much anything the urban sports enthusiast could ask for: a golf club with a netted driving range and swing simulators, a sleek bowling alley with 40 lanes; well-maintained facilities for soccer, basketball, rock climbing, ice skating, gymnastics, and basketball; and a super-deluxe health club complete with a competition-size swimming pool. The Spa at Chelsea Piers Is a sybarite's dream, with a wide selection of massage and dermatological services. Meanwhile, the Maritime Center offers a number of aquatic adventures, from a sailing school to harbor cruises. Non-athletes aren't entirely left out, either; there are a few dining options, including the picturesque Chelsea Brewing Company, which offers 20 handcrafted beers and marvelous harbor-side seating (including 100 al fresco seats). But really, there's no finer place to break a sweat.

SWIMMING POOLS

While none of the public pools are serene per se (as youth groups and diversion-seeking nannies favor them for youngsters), they do the trick; they are wet. Here are three spots that will take the heat off.

Hamilton Fish, 128 Pitt Street (Stanton), Lower East Side
Tel: 212 242 5228

John Jay, E 77th Street (York Ave), Upper East Side
Tel: 212 794 6566

Tony Dapolito Recreation Center, 1 Clarkson Street (7th Ave), West Village
Tel: 212 242 5228

TOURS

Gray Line All Loops Bus Tour, 777 Eighth Avenue (W 47th St), Midtown West
Tel: 212 445 0848   www.grayline.com

Allowing for 48 hours of unlimited hop-on, hop-off access to classic double-decker buses, the New York Sightseeing tours have four loops – Uptown, Downtown, Brooklyn, and a night-time tour that travels from Chinatown up to Rockefeller Center and over to the Empire State Building. These entertaining excursions are overseen by boisterous tour guides, who love to share their intricate knowledge.

Manhattan TV and Movie Sites/Sex & the City Hotspots/Sopranos Sites, various starting points
Tel: 212 209 3370   www.sceneontv.com

These three tours from On Location Tours, a company started by a plucky Skidmore grad in the mid-1990s, puts out-of-towners in touch with their celluloid dreams. The first goes everywhere from the Cosby Show town-house to the Ghostbusters firehouse to the Friends apartment building. The second conjures all the girlie glamour of *Sex & the City*, bouncing groups of girlfriends around to retrieve Magnolia Bakery's cupcakes, sit on Carrie Bradshaw's stoop, and grab a pink Martini at a bar from the show. The third gives wise guys a close-up look at the gritty spots featured on *The Sopranos*. If you love your boob tube, even on vacation, these are for you.

New York Gallery Tours, 526 West 26th Street (10th Ave), Chelsea
Tel: 212 946 1548 www.nygallerytours.com

If you know you want to hit some great galleries but have no clue how to begin, these contemporary art tours are a smart way to start. On each two-hour jaunt, customers take in eight different exhibits that include painting, video and mixed media, sculpture, and more. There are specific tours for gays and lesbians for a same-sex mingle factor, plus private tours can be arranged.

Times Square Tour, 42nd Street (Broadway), Midtown West
Tel: 212 768 1560

There's much to learn and see around New York's nerve center, a.k.a. Times Square. While it's presently a clean, tourist-friendly stretch, it was once the deliciously seedy center of big city depravity (and truth be told, a lot of locals miss that element). Of course, Broadway enthusiasts will love this up-close look at the Great White Way, and city planning fans will get a kick out of learning what's next for the neighborhood.

ZOOS AND AQUARIUMS

The Bronx Zoo/Wildlife Conservation Park, Bronx River Parkway (Fordham), The Bronx
Tel: 718 367 1010 www.bronxzoo.com
Open: daily, 10am–5pm (5.30pm Sat, Sun and holidays)

Opened in 1899, this incredible wildlife preserve – the largest metropolitan zoo in America – is home to more than 4,000 animals, on over 250 acres of land. Made humane and eco-friendly by the pioneers at the Wildlife Conservation Society, this much-loved attraction has an extraordinary cross section of beasts, insects, and reptiles, spread out in "natural environments" such as the Himalayan Highlands Habitat (snow leopards, white-necked cranes, red pandas), the Congo Gorilla Forest, and Tiger Mountain. You'll need (and want) an entire day to cover the zoo's vast offerings, so bring plenty of sunscreen and be prepared not to smoke.

Central Park Zoo/Wildlife Gallery, 830 Fifth Avenue (E 64th St), Upper East Side
Tel: 212 439 6500   www.centralpark.com
Open: daily, 10am–5pm (5.30pm Sat/Sun); during winter daily, 10am–4.30pm

The first major metropolitan zoo and "wildlife gallery" to ditch inhumane conditions and construct natural habitats for its animals, this marvelous zoo – home to penguins, polar bears, rare monkeys, piranhas, toads, bats, boars, and much more – is a subsidiary of the Wildlife Conservation Society, and a great way to spend the day. The Tisch Children's Zoo allows little guys to get up next to their favorite barnyard animals.

New York Aquarium, 602 Surf Avenue, Brooklyn
Tel: 718 265 3474   www.nyaquarium.com
Open: 10am–from 4.30pm to 7pm, depending on the time of year

Inhabiting 14 acres at world-famous Coney Island, the city's only aquarium houses over 8,000 creatures – including walruses, sea otters, octopuses, fish, and sharks – and conducts laboratory research as part of the Wildlife Conservation Society. Kids love the Aquatheater where California sea lions put on shows, and Beluga whales are just plain fascinating to any and all spectators. Follow up your stay with a few hours at Coney Island, taking in the public beach, Nathan's hot dogs, eye-popping boardwalk culture, and Astroland Park and its Cyclone (the world-famous wooden rollercoaster opened in 1927).

Prospect Park Zoo, 450 Flatbush Avenue, Brooklyn
Tel: 718 399 7339   www.prospectpark.org
Open: 10am–5pm (5.30pm Sat/Sun); during winter daily, 10am–4.30pm

Operated by the Wildlife Conservation Society, as are the Central Park and Queens zoos, this up-close-and-personal zoo is home to over 80 species of animals, from red pandas, sea lions, and exotic birds to prairie dogs and wallabies (both of which can be eyed-up face to face). This is the third incarnation of the Prospect Park Zoo, which opened in 1993 as a modern and humane habitat that replaced the cages and pits of yore. Very eco-forward and great for educating kids.

Notes & Updates

info...

DRESSING

New York is a place where anything can happen, so dress for it! You'll be walking a ton, so keep a comfy set of shoes handy.

DRIVING

Mass transit and taxis are always the rule of thumb in New York, since parking and traffic are often harrying experiences. If you have to get behind the wheel (a weekend jaunt to the Hamptons, antiquing in Connecticut, perhaps), you just have to give in to the flow of city driving. Taxi and bus drivers are a bold lot, weaving in and out of lanes with ferocity; you cannot turn right on a red light; and remember to heed street signs about left-hand turns during business days since there are restrictions throughout Midtown. Canal Street is always jam-packed due to entrances for the Holland Tunnel (towards New Jersey) and the Manhattan Bridge, so consider yourself warned. Watch for street-cleaning regulations when parking and, most importantly, jay-walkers – seasoned drivers expect a bold pedestrian or bike rider to appear out of nowhere, so be aware!

MONEY

New York is not cheap but it sure is fun. There are banks creeping up on most city corners, and the pervasive 24-hour delis around town usually have ATM machines. Just as the average American only speaks English, American businesses accept no currency other than the US dollar. Travelers' checks are always a good way to go.

NAVIGATION

Getting around New York's numbered streets and avenues is easy. They are arranged in a grid; just pay attention to West and East designations. (East 23rd Street is to the east of Fifth Avenue, West 23rd Street is to the west of Fifth Avenue. It's that simple.) Broadway is confusing, for it slices in a subtle diagonal line through the city – it is on the west side of the city uptown all the way to 23rd Street, then finds itself on the east side of the city. Then, of course, there are the fabled cowpaths-turned-streets of the West Village, and the named streets

i

info...

below Houston Street. Invest in a great, detailed city map, such as the Streetwise series (Streetwisemaps.com).

PUBLIC HOLIDAYS

In this city of frenetic commerce and industry, many people tend to work right through their public holidays. But then again, many don't. Worry not, however... You can always find an open restaurant or deli, even on Christmas Day. The North American public holidays, according to the US bank holiday calendar, are: New Year's Day (1 January), Martin Luther King, Jr. Day (third Monday of January), President's Day (third Monday of February), Good Friday (Friday before Easter), Memorial Day (last Monday of May), Independence Day (4 July), Labor Day (first Monday in September), Columbus Day (12 October), Veteran's Day (11 November), Thanksgiving Day (fourth Thursday of November), Christmas Day (25 December).

PUBLIC TRANSPORTATION

The New York subway system gets a bad rap when really it's one of the most intricate, fascinating, and efficient transportation networks in the world. Still, it's intimidating. Just know that the dangerous, graffiti-laden system from the movies isn't how it is today; well-lit cars are getting more modern by the month, and nowhere is the people-watching better. (Truly, you'll never see such a mix of cultures peaceably coexisting.) Track work on the weekends and at night can occasionally cause trains to be re-routed, so keep an eye out for signs or ask the attendants. (Or, hey, ask a stranger... New Yorkers – contrary to popular belief – are some of the friendliest, most helpful folks you'll meet, and love to show off their knowledge of the city.) Similarly, city buses are surprisingly clean and efficient; you just have to know what numbers to look for.

SMOKING

Smoking in public spaces is a thing of the past, so prepare to light up outside your restaurant or bar (or in specially designated al fresco smoking sections). Also, the average pack of smokes sells for $7–8. While some find the smoking ban frustrating, most New Yorkers – even regular smokers – agree that it's nice to be able to go out for an evening and not come home reeking of cigarettes.

TAXIS

Taxis are usually the fastest way to get around town. Stick your hand out and hail one over – just don't steal another person's cab, or you'll feel the consequences. You can't smoke in them, so don't try, and no more than four people are allowed in a cab. A cab is occupied when the sign on top of the car is not lit up. It is off duty when the two side lights are lit on the top of the car (they're not just ignoring you). The fare is calculated based on a combination of time spent and distance covered. There is an initial charge of $2.50, with $.40 per fifth of a mile, $.40 per 60 seconds, a $1 surcharge between 4pm and 8pm and a $.50 surcharge between 8pm and 6am. Bring cash (although some have begun accepting credit cards). To get to Newark International Airport, there is the metered rate plus a $15 surcharge, plus tolls. For John F. Kennedy International Airport, there is a flat fee of $45 plus any tolls, from Manhattan. For LaGuardia International Airport, passengers pay the regular meter rate.

TELEPHONES

To dial New York from out of the country, dial 00 + 1 + 212 before your number. If dialing from within the United States or Canada, simply dial 1 + 212 and then your number.

TIPPING

Bartenders, waiters, and taxi drivers make the substantive portions of their incomes from tips. For taxis, it is customary to round up to the nearest dollar and add an extra dollar, though that depends on the service and length of the ride. (For longer rides, give a bit more.) For excellent service in a restaurant or bar, give 20%. For so-so service, the customary tip is 15%. For maid service, leave $3 for every time they clean the room. For hairdressers or massage therapists, give 15–20%. For doormen who hail you a cab, give a dollar.

info...

Notes & Updates

Hg2 New York

index

index

index